Praise for *Running*

"What a fantastic story this is! Pamela shares her personal experiences with such love and inspiration as she discovers the unchanging principle of the 'law of the harvest.' What a motivating, practical read!"

Dr. Stephen R. Covey, author
The 7 Habits of Highly Effective People and *The 8th Habit: From Effectiveness to Greatness*

"The story that Pam Hansen tells is both tragic and heartwarming. Not only did she discover that stress is the most common cause of obesity, she learned that exercise is the foundation of any successful weight-loss program. The way she overcame both personal and familial problems is truly remarkable. This is a 'must-read' for anyone fighting obesity."

Kenneth H. Cooper, MD, MPH
Chairman & CEO, Cooper Clinic, Dallas, Texas,
and bestselling health and fitness author

"*Running with Angels* is a powerful, personal story that demonstrates the power of strong social support, positive focusing, empowerment, and falling back in love with a body she had grown to despise. I highly recommend *Running with Angels* to anyone struggling with any type of health problem."

Keith J. Karren, Ph.D.
Professor, Health Science Department, Brigham Young University

"I have rarely read anything that more clearly communicates true understanding of the pains and struggles of life than what Pam Hansen has written in this book. Although it deals with overcoming obesity, it easily translates into so many other challenges in life. She is remarkably open and honest, and I greatly admire her and her remarkable journey of courage. I commend it to anyone who struggles with anything."

Dr. Jim MacArthur
Psychologist and author of *Everyday Parents Raising Great Kids*

"Pam's story is uplifting and inspiring. Her insights into life and overcoming obesity are powerful and thought-provoking. This is a wonderful book for anyone suffering from obesity or other significant challenges."

Larry Tucker, Ph.D.
Professor, Department of Exercise Sciences
Brigham Young University

"*Running with Angels* is one of the most unique books I've read in a long time. It applies to so many different pockets of people, from runners, to grieving families, to those with weight issues. Everyone will be inspired by Pam's triumphs over her lifelong struggles."

Heather Walker
Bereavement Specialist, Utah Valley Regional Medical Center

"*Running with Angels* is a book you can't put down! Pam Hansen tells a tender, compelling story in this very personal account of the loss of her children as a young mother . . . and loss of self. From the hurtful comments that come with obesity to the euphoria of crossing a marathon finish line, Pam takes us on a journey that makes you want to stand and cheer . . . then lace up your running shoes!"

Sammy Linebaugh
Reporter, KSL-TV (NBC affiliate, Salt Lake City, Utah)

"Helen Keller told us that the world is full of sorrow and the overcoming of sorrow. This book presents one realistic, forthright example. *Running with Angels* is frank, authentic, and inspiring. I recommend it for anyone who grieves, or diets, or runs, or who wants an encouraging view of human capacity."

Dianne Nielsen, Ph.D.
Clinical psychologist and runner

"Pam Hansen pulled me in from the very first page of *Running with Angels*. I wrote down several of her inspirational quotes so I could use them as my own daily motivation. I empathized strongly with her descriptions of the frustration and heartache associated with her children's disabilities as I reflected on my own experiences of raising two daughters with spina bifida."

Melodie Bestor
Chairperson, English Department, Orem High School

Running
with Angels

Running with Angels

*The Inspiring Journey of a Woman
Who Turned Personal Tragedy into Triumph
Over Obesity*

Pamela H. Hansen

SHADOW
MOUNTAIN

To my beloved angels—
Mark, Nicholas, Emily, Amy, Sarah,
Stephen, Hillary, and Eric

Library of Congress Cataloging-in-Publication Data

Hansen, Pamela H.
  Running with angels / Pamela H. Hansen.
     p.   cm.
  ISBN 1-59038-381-8 (pbk.)
  1. Overweight women—United States—Biography.   2. Marathon running.
3. Women runners—United States—Biography.   I. Title.
RC552.O25H36 2004
362.196'398'0092—dc22
                                                                  2004020818

Printed in the United States of America   54459
Malloy Lithographing Incorporated, Ann Arbor, MI

10   9   8   7   6   5   4   3

Contents

Acknowledgments

My heartfelt thanks go to the staff at Shadow Mountain—working with product director Jana Erickson has been an absolute joy! She has been so positive and has shown such support and patience. My editor, Richard Peterson, has been very helpful and kind, and I have especially enjoyed his good humor. I have also enjoyed getting to know publicist Gail Halladay and am grateful for her enthusiasm and hard work. I am thankful too for the talents of Richard Erickson, art director; Scott Eggers, designer; and Tonya Facemyer, typographer.

In the book, I could not mention all the compassionate doctors who have provided loving care to our family and have helped us better understand the medical world. Special gratitude goes to James Lamoreaux, M.D.; David Johnson, M.D.; John Bohnsack, M.D. and his associate, Marion Szewczyk, RNCMSN; Barry Myones, M.D.; along with Michael Abrams, M.D.; and R. Lor Randall, M.D. Others who deserve recognition include:

Stuart Slingerland, M.D.; Richard Lohner, M.D.; Kent Gamette, M.D.; Howard Francis, M.D.; and Brent Lind, M.D.

I will be forever grateful to Dale G. Johnson, M.D. for his loving concern, as well as his astute knowledge of pediatrics. Tears still come to my eyes when I think about the occasion he and his wife, my dear Aunt Beverly, stopped long enough to visit with us, which literally changed our daughter Sarah's future.

In writing this book, I have also come to understand more fully the value of friendship. I could not have done it without the help of so many wonderful friends. Lisa Warnick and Ginger Fisher have always been there, cheering me on. Greg and Janet Taggart offered tremendous encouragement in the beginning of this project. I appreciate their support at such a critical time. Camille Buhman offered many hours of time and effort in helping me organize my thoughts. Lee Perry and Rosemary Olsen also provided valuable insights. My friend Karen Cope did a beautiful job with the professional photography in the book. And Sammy Linebaugh from KSL-TV quickly became a delightful friend of our whole family. She has been kind and sensitive in helping to share my story. There are also others, too many to mention, who have blessed our lives and been so supportive. Thanks to all of you.

My dear uncle Gordon T. Allred taught me how to breathe more life into my writing. I kept a box of tissues close as I struggled to inscribe this story, reliving many of the memories in more detail as a result of his tender tutelage.

My in-laws, Jerry and Margaret Hansen, as well as the rest of the Hansen family, have been incredibly supportive of this project. I love you and am eternally grateful to be part of your family.

My parents, Robert and Carolee Harmon, and my adorable,

97-year-old grandmother, LeOra C. Larsen, have taught me how essential it is to have faith and an optimistic outlook as we experience trials. I love each of you!

I also express my love for my siblings and their families—David and Nancy Harmon, Chris and Tyler Sheffield, Jill Harmon, and Holly and Bryan Webster. Their support and comments about the book have been incredibly helpful.

My husband, Mark, has always loved me regardless of my dress size. I am delighted to be by his side. We discussed this manuscript late into countless nights and throughout innumerable morning walks. He tirelessly read multiple versions of each chapter time and again. Writing is an important part of his professional life, and on several occasions I wanted him to take over and write this book for me. Although he offered valuable suggestions, he always told me that this needed to be "my story." I now realize that writing this book has been like most of the truly meaningful experiences in life—although others can help, share, and support, there is no substitute for first-hand experience. I appreciate Mark's continued patience, love, acceptance, and gentle encouragement. I love sharing life with you, sweetheart!

I am grateful for our beloved children, Nicholas, Amy, Sarah, Stephen, and Hillary. I appreciate your patience and support during my work on this book. What a thrill it is to watch you experience life. I truly love being your mother!

Finally, I express my profound gratitude for a wise and loving Father in Heaven. I believe He has a plan for all of us. I am thankful for my precious little angels, Emily and Eric. In my heart and mind, they have been with me every step of the way. Because of them, the miracle in this story has come to pass.

Summer 1998

Eating fudge, January 2000

My daughters in my "before" pants

Trying to keep up with the sled, December 2000

Supportive friends, July 2002

Pam's family at the cemetery

At mile 19, Salt Lake Marathon, 24 July 2002

Pam with her family after completing the St. George Marathon in 2003

Pam Hansen, 2004

CHAPTER ONE

An Angel Daughter

July 24, 2002, 3:30 A.M. The buses waited in the cool
darkness of the early morning. As I got out of the car, I looked
up at the blanket of brightly shining stars in the clear sky. Was
I actually here? I glanced over at my husband, Mark. We had
talked about this moment for so many years—running the
Deseret News Marathon—and doing it together. Now that it
was actually happening, it seemed almost surreal.

The buses would leave shortly to take the runners up the
canyon to the starting line. Cars continued to pull into the
University of Utah parking lot at Rice-Eccles Stadium,
where, only a few months earlier at the Winter Olympics,
athletes from all over the world had marched and waved to
cheering spectators. This was certainly a place of hope and
anticipation.

And today was no different. Runners prepared themselves as they drank Gatorade and made last-minute

adjustments of their running attire. Some even took advantage of the various porta-potties that were set up specifically for this event. I wondered if the buses could have parked just a bit further away from them, as their massive headlights spotlighted the bathroom doors as nervous runners ducked in and out before boarding.

The bus Mark and I boarded was almost full. In fact, the only two remaining seats, though not together, were across the aisle from one another, toward the back. I had goose bumps from the excitement and the cold as I walked down the aisle to my seat. I wondered if I should bring my sweatshirt or leave it back in the car. I would only need its warmth for another hour or so, and then I would be glad I didn't have it. Officials had given us a bag to put our stuff in just before the race would start. I decided to take my sweatshirt along.

I also wondered if I should have worn something else on my legs, over my black spandex shorts. I smiled as I realized that just a few years ago I wouldn't have even dared to wear shorts around the house, let alone tight spandex in public! I knew the scorching heat would arrive in a few short hours, and I would be glad to be wearing the clothes I had on, even if it meant a bit of shivering before the race. I loved the baby blue color of my Nike shirt; it was soft and happy. I wiggled my toes around in my shoes, making sure they had lots of room. My socks had never given me blisters before, even on long runs, and I hoped they would give me the same protection that morning. As I sat down, I adjusted my fanny pack, which held my tape player, favorite running songs that I would listen to when I wasn't listening to Mark, and three packs of awful-tasting carbohydrate gel that would hopefully give me a few needed boosts. Yes, my "list" was there, too. I carefully folded it and put it in the pocket of my shorts. A few nights before, I had written down the names of all those who had helped me get that far. I wanted to "dedicate" a mile of the marathon to each one of them. Compiling the list had been an emotional experience, as I realized how many angels there were in my life.

The bus finally pulled away from the safety and comfort of the parking lot and was soon on its way up the canyon. I looked over at Mark, who was visiting with an older man sitting next to him. Mark wore running clothes similar to mine, with the same spandex shorts, and a deep blue T-shirt. I was so glad he was there, too. We had been on many training runs together, and although they were always better with him beside me, I knew he had to run at a slower pace with me along. He had already run this marathon twice before, each time vowing never to do it again. I was about to find out why.

My thoughts turned to our children. They had spent the night at my parents' home in Salt Lake City, an hour from our home in Orem. To avoid the heat of the day, the race was to begin at 5:00 A.M. To allow for adequate time to stretch and make the bus ride to the starting area, Mark and I awakened at 2:00 A.M., which didn't allow much time for sleep. Mark had drifted off rather quickly, but I must have checked the clock every ten minutes throughout the night. I did not sleep at all. I felt like a child on Christmas Eve, full of excitement and anticipation. I had dreamed of running this marathon for twenty years, and now it was finally here!

Sitting next to me was a man about my same age. He had plenty of running stories and was willing to share them all with me. I heard other runners talking and comparing marathon memories. Some shared injury reports and incredible race times. There was also talk of shoes and running gear.

I looked around the bus. In the darkness, I could faintly make out runners listening to music through their headphones or trying to catch a final nap as the bus crept up the hill. I knew that for each mile I sat comfortably in the nice cozy bus, I would have to run back down the canyon, using my own strength. For a moment, I thought of stowing away in the back of the bus.

The man next to me rambled on, telling me how he was going to run the "Grand Slam" this year, which consisted of completing all five major Utah marathons in one year—beginning with the Ogden Marathon in May, the Park City Marathon in June, the Salt Lake, or *Deseret News* Marathon, as some called it, in July, the Top of Utah Marathon in Logan during September, and culminating with the St. George Marathon in October. I thought he was crazy. But then again, there were those who had told me I was crazy to be running any marathon, let alone *this* one. This was considered to be one of the most difficult in the country, because of all the hills, high altitude, and heat.

Yet my dream lived on, ever since it began years earlier, when I volunteered for this event and watched as the runners came across the finish line, their faces full of triumph. I wanted to experience that. And now, because of the events of the past few years, running this marathon signified much more than a dream. It had evolved into a glorious commemoration as well, for just a year and a half earlier, I had weighed one hundred pounds more than I did that day. Every step of those 26.2 miles that I was to run that morning, I would be immensely grateful for a chance of renewal. I would also be celebrating life itself—observing triumph over tragedy, marveling at the miracle of exercise, the incredible effects of weight loss, and the power of prayer, and rejoicing that families can be eternal.

I closed my eyes and leaned back against the headrest, reflecting back thirteen years, when my journey had begun.

"You're having twins!" the doctor announced with a toothy grin, as he performed the ultrasound. Mark and I looked at each other. Was he serious? He wasn't just kidding because my stomach measured bigger than it was supposed to be, and I was only halfway through the pregnancy? Yet there they were—we could see *two* babies on the ultrasound screen. The nurse even stepped over for a closer look as the small examination room seemed to swirl around me. I reached for Mark's hand, which was surprisingly even sweatier than mine was, and I squinted my eyes to see every little detail as the doctor pointed them out. The babies looked so adorable already! We were thrilled to discover they were both girls. I wished we could have stayed there all afternoon, just watching them interact. All too soon, though, the exam was finished, and Mark helped me up from the table, both of us feeling a little weak from all the excitement.

I was sure the entire waiting room could hear my heart thumping as we stopped at the front desk to make my next appointment. We could hardly wait to get home to share the news with Nicholas.

Our son, Nicholas, was two years old, and was eager to have two little sisters arrive at the same time. Having watched me throw up almost every day, he was well aware that I was pregnant. He was concerned, though I often reassured him that

"Mommy is okay, she just has an upset stomach again." And "No, the babies won't get thrown up." Other than the extreme nausea, the pregnancy was what the doctor considered "uneventful." The increased discomfort was bearable as I thought about holding and cuddling those two little girls in a few months.

Because of the danger of premature labor, we spent many weeks trying to prevent the babies from coming too soon. The doctor told me to stay in bed as much as possible, so Nicholas stayed with his grandparents for a few weeks. I missed him terribly, but I knew he was having a great time. Mark was a first year MBA student at Brigham Young University, which required him to study long hours. During that time, I read all the books I could find about raising twins. I could see it would not be easy, but I was anxiously awaiting the opportunity.

During the seventh month of pregnancy, we visited Stephen Clark, M.D., a neonatologist at Utah Valley Hospital, for an indepth ultrasound, routinely performed with twin pregnancies. My back ached as soon as it touched the table, trying to hold up all the extra weight. However, as the doctor slid the cold ultrasound sensor through the gooey gel all around my protruding belly, the pain seemed to subside as I watched these little ones intertwine. Dr. Clark and his nurse highlighted and recorded measurements of both babies, and I realized that for them, this was just another day at the office. However, for Mark and me, it was as if we were getting an early peek at a much-anticipated gift.

I was amazed how thoroughly Dr. Clark examined each twin, labeling them "Twin A" and "Twin B." "Twin A," or Amy, as she would come to be known, was the smaller of the two. She was upright, on my left side. Mark and I named "Twin B" Emily.

She was, Dr. Clark told us, in the more desirable position, which was head down, on the right side, and she had a healthier looking placenta.

I eagerly counted ten little fingers and toes on each baby, and felt relief as I saw each perfectly formed body part. The doctor pointed out the developing brains, spines, kidneys, and lungs, and even with my untrained eye, I could distinguish them. The babies seemed caught between playing together and finding a way in which they could be comfortable. Their little arms reached out for one another, then they kicked and squirmed some more. They even sucked their thumbs. A feeling of anticipation swept over me, and we were mesmerized as we watched all the movement that I had felt all these months. We also more fully understood why I had not been able to sleep much.

As the exam continued, the doctor looked quite closely at Emily. He moved the sensor around, taking measurements, then he returned to the same place—her heart. I could see from his expression that he was uneasy, and I searched his face for answers. He wore a sober expression, and at times leaned forward, scrunching his eyebrows, trying to get a better look. Mark and I kept looking at each other, trying to make sense of what might be happening. Neither of us dared speak. The excited, euphoric feeling began to fade. Dr. Clark told us that he wanted me to get up and walk around the hospital for about forty-five minutes to enable the babies to move into another position, where he could get a better look at them. A feeling of panic swept over me. Couldn't he see just fine? Was he stalling? Was there something he needed to tell us? We were too scared to ask him anything. We just kept hoping everything would be fine.

The forty-five minute walk was the longest Mark and I had

ever taken. We wandered around in a daze, with all sorts of thoughts running through our heads. Every so often one of us wondered aloud if there was a hole in her heart, or some other defect requiring surgery or extensive therapy. We felt determined that we would do all we could to help her through whatever it was, so that she could be healthy and live as full a life as possible.

We arrived back in the doctor's examination room, where we met a solemn-looking doctor. Squeezing out the sticky goo on my stomach once again, he proceeded with his examination. Little Emily had moved to a different position, and he was able to see things more clearly this time. It didn't take him long to finish. He forced a slight but sad smile as he told us to meet him down the hall in his office. I trembled as Mark helped me down from the table. We sensed something was terribly wrong as we made what seemed like a long, almost surreal walk to his office. We sat down on one side of Dr. Clark's desk as he sat on the other, folding his hands in front of him while leaning forward ever so slightly. I watched his fingers interlock so I could avoid the poignant expression on his face. He got right to the point. For the second time during that pregnancy, we heard unexpected news that would change us forever. He gently said, "One of your babies has a condition that is incompatible with life." *What?* Mark and I looked at each other. Had we heard him correctly? Did he say, *"Incompatible with life"?* That could only mean . . .

Everything he said after that all ran together. I faintly heard him explain that Emily had Hypoplastic Left Heart Syndrome, a condition in which the left side of the heart is either under-developed or simply nonexistent. Since the mother pumps blood for the baby during pregnancy, the baby is able to grow and develop an otherwise healthy body. However, just after birth, when the baby is required to pump blood with her own heart, without the left side working, blood cannot flow to her body, resulting in death. I quit listening after that, unable to process any more. I felt sick. It was as if someone had taken a huge club and pummeled me in the stomach.

We were in shock. This could not be happening! Emily looked so flawless. She was the bigger twin, with the healthier placenta, and all her little parts looked so perfectly formed. It seemed impossible to me that she truly had such a fatal heart defect. Maybe the doctor could not see very well, even with that second exam. Although he *said* they were in a position where he could see them well, maybe he just could not see well *enough*. Although he was supposed to be one of the best neonatologists in the intermountain area, he was still human—wasn't he capable of making a mistake? It just couldn't be true. Other than the nausea and early contractions, everything else during the pregnancy had seemed perfectly normal. So many times we had heard both heartbeats so clearly and rhythmically. No, there must be some error. We just sat there, trying to make some sense out of what the doctor was telling us, too shocked to fully comprehend the news.

Dr. Clark wanted us to see another neonatologist at nearby Primary Children's Hospital, in Salt Lake City, where there was an even more elaborate ultrasound machine than the one we had just used, where the actual blood flow of each baby could be tracked.

As we walked out of the hospital that day, we hoped that somehow this was just a cruel misdiagnosis. On the drive home, I looked at people coming and going. Life had not seemed to change. Men and women were driving to work, mothers were hurrying children in and out of grocery stores, and people were filling their cars with gas. I was amazed that life was continuing, even though my world was breaking apart.

A few days later, after Mark and I had spent hours reviewing our visit with Dr. Clark, we arrived at our appointment with Gregory DeVore, M.D., full of hope. We had been praying for a miracle. However, we also had a very uneasy feeling that we were not going to get the miracle we wanted.

Mark helped me onto the examination table. I moved slowly, not just because I was so heavy, but I hoped that if I didn't move around too much, Emily's heart could somehow finish its needed growth, and she would be fine.

It wasn't long before a very kind and sympathetic Dr. DeVore confirmed the diagnosis. Emily was not expected to live long.

I was glad I was lying down. My whole body felt like Jell-O. I was so weak I could barely sit up after the exam. Mark helped me back to the doctor's office where we slowly sat down on his couch. Dr. DeVore pulled his chair closer to us. I had already shed so many tears since the initial diagnosis, but the floodgates opened yet again. In his grief, Mark was so tender and could not do much more than simply put his arm around me. He gently rubbed my shoulder as the doctor reiterated what we already knew.

But now we wanted to know more. We inundated the doctor with questions, desperately searching for a way we could save our daughter. No one, we were told, knew exactly how long babies with this condition would live. It all depended on how long the patent ductus arteriosus stayed open. This, he explained, was a small part of the heart, present in every baby, which naturally stayed open for days or weeks after birth, and allowed blood to flow freely throughout the body. However, when the duct naturally closed, each side of the heart would have to begin performing its own function. Without the essential left side, the heart would not be able to operate properly.

Dr. DeVore went on to tell us that this particular heart defect occurred once in every 10,000 births. It was even rarer in a twin. The cause was unknown, and there was no cure, other than a heart transplant. At the time, only a few transplants had been successfully performed on infants, but because of her small size, the likelihood of even finding a heart tiny enough to fit into her little five-pound body, not to mention the minute window of time we had, was close to nonexistent. Smaller still was the possibility she would even survive the surgery. I felt as if my own heart was breaking as the certainty of our baby's condition was finally sinking in.

We left the hospital in silence. It was a cold January day, and the dreary weather reflected my emotions. Once again, life went on around us, but our world seemed to have stopped. Mark and I considered the options. The first, as it was explained to us, was to "do nothing, but let nature take its course." We were assured they would do all they could to get both babies here safely, then we would be able to "enjoy" Emily for as long as she could stay. The only other possible option was for us to move to California (for an extended period, to allow for follow-up care), where I would deliver the babies at Loma Linda University Hospital, the only place, at the time, that infant heart transplants were being done. There, Emily would be stabilized as much as possible to wait for a heart, which, we were reminded, had a next-to-zero chance of even being found.

Just weeks before, Mark and I had been discussing the challenges we would face in having three children under the age of three, living in a small two-bedroom apartment, and finishing graduate school. Now, instead of studying and preparing for his next research paper, Mark was trying to help me decide if we should try drastic measures to save our daughter's young life. I still wanted desperately to be "worrying" about how I was going to make it through those first difficult twelve months with twins, as I had read about in all those books. Now those challenges seemed easy, as we considered our baby daughter's survival.

We did not have much time to make our decision and spent most of the next few days considering the options and even more time praying. I just wanted someone to tell me what we should do. I wanted a crystal ball to show me what the outcome of each decision would be, hours, days, weeks, and years down the road.

The choice was one no parent should have to make. I thought of the many times during the pregnancy that I had been asked, "Do you want two boys, two girls, or one of each?" My response had been, "It doesn't matter, as long as they are healthy!" Now guilt also added to my burden, although I realized my answer reflected more flippancy than how I truly felt. In fact, I had never given much thought to the possibility that I would ever have a baby with problems.

The final weeks of pregnancy were full of heartache, hope, prayer, and tears. Mark carried an incredible burden as he tried to do well in his classes, deal with a pregnant, bedridden wife as well as an active toddler, while preparing for the birth—and death—of our daughters. He was a tremendous comfort to me. I was glad his professors had the charity and willingness to give him extra time to finish his assignments.

Although we felt comforted, we still agonized about our

decision. There were many "What ifs?" that crossed our minds. Nevertheless, although the pain and heartache were still there, our belief that families can be together forever shed a clearer light on things and became a tremendous comfort.

After an incredible amount of thought, discussion, and prayer, we opted not to attempt the transplant. Although in our hearts we continued to pray for that last-minute miracle, we felt a surprising sense of peace with our decision. We felt strongly that what was to happen after our daughter's birth was the will of a loving Father in Heaven. Although we continued to hope for a miracle and knew without a doubt that one was possible, we also felt that she was not meant to live long on the earth. It was to be one of the most humbling lessons we would ever learn.

The next weeks included checkups and non-stress tests, since the premature contractions adversely affected Amy. I was also very concerned about her, especially as I realized what she must be experiencing, too. The contractions affected Emily as well, but the doctors and technicians did not record her reactions to the tests. I was grateful for Amy's apparent good health, but heartbroken to think they had abandoned Emily, and after a few of the tests, I tearfully asked the technician to please check and see how she was doing, too. Her heartbeat continued to sound so steady and strong that it still seemed unfathomable that her heart would not be capable of keeping her alive on its own.

Carrying multiple babies meant multiple challenges. The added weight and strain on my body greatly increased the discomfort. For me, being pregnant with twins was like experiencing all the symptoms of a single pregnancy—multiplied by two. I encountered extreme nausea throughout the entire pregnancy, and the backaches, the bathroom breaks, the cravings, and certainly, the expansion of my abdomen—all seemed to be at least twice what they were with my first pregnancy. A friend once told me that one of the only reasons women are pregnant that last month is so we will do anything—even go through the incredible pains of labor—to deliver the baby and be free from the discomfort that last month brings!

Up until we discovered Emily's heart defect, I looked forward with great anticipation to the delivery of these babies. However, the more I realized what was to happen after they were born, the more I wanted to stay pregnant for as long as I could. I knew that while Emily stayed inside, with my heart pumping her blood, she could survive. It is a strange feeling, wanting to be pregnant forever.

Then, on February 3, 1989, during a non-stress test, it was determined that, even though the babies weren't due for another four weeks, the stress on Amy was increasing, and a cesarean section needed to be performed immediately. Once that decision was made, everything moved very quickly.

Mark helped me to the bed as the nurse came to wheel me into the operating room. I felt weak; the nightmare was unfolding. Soon I began to shiver, almost uncontrollably. The nurse covered me with warm blankets, and then hooked up an IV. An anesthesiologist came in to administer the epidural. It seemed as though most of the other hospital personnel were there in the room, too. Doctors and nurses were everywhere, each bustling about with a special mission to perform. Everything seemed to move in a blur, while outside, snow had been softly falling for hours. The streets were clogged with white powder and slush, and I vaguely heard one of the doctors remark to another how difficult it had been to get down his steep neighborhood street to the hospital. He said he had been having a discussion with his son about who was going to take the Suburban that morning. As he went about preparing for the surgery, talking about dealing with his teenager, once again I realized that although the events of that morning would forever change our family's lives, they were routine in the life of a doctor.

Just after noon, Emily was born. I immediately noticed her purplish color. A few years earlier, when Nicholas was born, he had a healthy, pink, robustness about him. Emily appeared markedly different. Already she was not getting the oxygen she needed. I wept as she uttered her first cry, not knowing how long I would be able to hear that lovely sound. I wanted everything else to stand still while I recorded that song in my heart.

Mark held my hand as a team of doctors and nurses stabilized Emily, and, as they had explained to us weeks before, prepared to take her to Primary Children's Hospital, about 45 miles away, where specialists would examine her more completely. I was only able to hold her for a few minutes and touch her soft little cheek to mine before they whisked her away. I wanted to memorize every moment. Although I was still in the process of delivering Amy by C-section, I wanted to remember as much of Emily's life as I could.

I cried with joy when I saw Amy. She looked so tiny and fragile, yet her color was a soft pink. She weighed just over four pounds, and was barely seventeen inches long. Her little mouth was just big enough to let out a delicate cry. Her tiny arms were flailing all around, grasping for the cozy warmth of the only home she had known and the sister who had shared it with her. I was only able to cuddle her for what seemed a few seconds before the doctors and nurses hurried her away to the Newborn Intensive Care Unit. I couldn't wait to hold her again.

Earlier that morning we had alerted our family members that the babies would be born soon. Mark's parents traveled from Idaho. My parents, sisters, and my beloved grandmother, for whom we gave Emily her middle name, LeOra, came from Salt Lake. Most were able to arrive quickly, and they stayed with me, which was tremendously comforting, while Mark went with Emily to Primary Children's Hospital. Because of the huge snowfall that morning, the roads were treacherous.

Doctors looked at Emily's heart through an ultrasound, and Mark called me soon after the exam. We had still been hoping and praying for that last minute miracle that we knew *could* happen . . . However, Mark sadly explained that the ultrasound had confirmed her fatal heart defect. They would bring her back to Provo.

It had now been a few hours since the babies' births. The pain medication was beginning to wear off, and I could feel the physical effects of the C-section. However, even as agonizing as that was, it did not compare to the sorrow that was engulfing my heart.

Soon after leaving the hospital in Salt Lake, Emily stopped breathing. The medical team quickly looked at Mark and asked him what he wanted them to do. Mark pleaded with them to do all they could to revive her. He told me later he wanted Emily to be able to die in her mother's arms, rather than there on the avenues of Salt Lake City. After some tense moments, a breathing tube was put down her little throat; she got the needed oxygen and continued to breathe. The ambulance traveled as quickly as it could over the snowpacked roads back to the hospital in Provo. All of our immediate family members who were able to be there had gathered by then. We were so grateful for our family's help and support at that time, particularly with caring for Nicholas during the previous few weeks.

Nicholas, in his little two-year-old mind, seemed to sense something was terribly wrong. He had been so excited for the arrival of his little sisters, and now they were finally here. Yet, he had seen his parents, who were usually happy and playful with him, shed many tears over the previous few weeks, and had observed many serious, subdued discussions between them. But on this day, he had both sets of grandparents, his great-grandmother, as well as aunts, uncles, and cousins, all at the hospital. He was thrilled they were all there together. He felt loved and happy to be with the most important people in his young life. Of course, he could not comprehend all that was happening. I thought at the time how wonderful it would be to have the simple perception of a two-year-old.

I wanted so much to have a family picture taken before Emily died. I thought about the pink, frilly dresses that I had bought for the girls just a few days earlier, on a rare outing away from the house, hoping to dress them for at least one nice family portrait. With Emily's labored breathing, however, I didn't want to do anything to cause her further discomfort. The dresses stayed in the shopping bag. Nicholas was wearing his favorite green sweatshirt, which had a big Santa Claus on the front. Amy was curled up in peaceful slumber with her little fist up against her cheek, and she looked like a cute little mouse, with a red bow in her hair. Emily, with a tiny pink bow in her dark, thick hair, continued to have the oxygen tube up against her nostrils, her tiny brow furrowed and a painful expression on her sweet little face. I wore the fashionable hospital gown, tears having washed away any trace of makeup on my face. My hair showed telltale signs of having been in bed for a month. Mark's eyes were swollen from crying and lack of sleep. We disregarded how we looked, and my dad took pictures. It was especially difficult for me to smile, and yet I knew this would be our only complete family portrait.

Soon after the photo session, Emily's breathing became much more labored. We heard her delicate little cries, as if she knew she was about to leave us. We gathered around the bed while Mark, along with both of our fathers, took Emily in their arms and gave her a father's blessing. He welcomed her to our eternal family and bade her a heart-wrenching good-bye for a lifetime. Soon after that, her breathing became even more labored. Our family members left the room, and we thought it was time for her to go. She had lived for almost eight hours. As we continued to hold her, we prayed that she would be comforted and we would be strengthened. We expressed love and appreciation for her. Although we knew she was an eternal part of our family, I could not deny the fact that I still wanted to hang on to her. I still wanted a miracle!

The nurses also left us alone with our daughter. Mark and I took turns holding her, as she continued to fight for every breath. As the minutes turned to hours, we felt as if we had been given a priceless gift of extra time with our baby. We talked peacefully to her and hoped she could feel the tremendous love we had for her. Through our tears we told her all about her adorable big brother, and that we would do our best raising her beautiful twin sister. I wanted to tell Emily every story, fairy tale, and poem I knew. I had built up quite a repertoire during the past few years, as I spent countless hours reading to Nicholas. I wanted to fit a lifetime of stories into a few precious moments, but now, as I held Emily in my arms, I could not recall a single one. I could only think of a few favorite lullabies, so I sang those, beginning with "Winkin', Blinkin', and Nod." She responded with a calmer expression. So I continued to sing, into the night. I also sang a few children's church songs to her, but I cried as I realized that she would not experience the joy I had felt in singing them.

A song that Janice Kapp Perry had written for her infant son would soon become one of my favorites. The lyrics of the chorus, adapted to my daughter, include:

> *And my heart sang a lullaby to celebrate birth,*
> *As she crossed the veil between heaven and earth.*
> *My heart sang a lullaby for this tiny one,*
> *A song of forever, of things yet to come—*
> *Just a lullaby to carry her home.*

I spoke softly to her as I tried to embed everything about her into my memory—her expressions, her delicate features, her every breath, her tiny, agonizing whimpers, and the way she wrapped her little hand around my finger. Mark and I continued to take turns holding her into the next morning as we tried to paint a picture of her in our hearts.

The next day was a beautiful, snowy Friday. As the morning wore on, we knew it was finally time for her to return home. I will forever remember her last earthly moments. Up until now she had been breathing quite rapidly, fighting for every little bit of oxygen her little body would allow. Now, it was as if her strength were gone, and she was finally ready to relinquish the fight. She had stayed longer than we had all thought she could. Those final few breaths were as if she were trying to tell us to be of good cheer; that we would all be together again someday. I felt love coming from her as I have never experienced at any other time in my life. It was a priceless moment, between mother and daughter, that I will cherish forever.

At 10:55 A.M. on February 4, 1989, Emily breathed her last. My heart felt as though it was truly breaking as we said good-bye. As Mark embraced us both, she died in my arms. Part of me went with her.

I took tremendous comfort in having a loving husband, as well as another baby to hold. But the sorrow and the loss were very real. We were also comforted by the concern and out-pouring of love from supportive family and friends.

Amy could not leave the Newborn Intensive Care Unit (NICU), except to spend a few moments with us. We spent most of our time with Emily that first day. It was an absolute roller coaster of emotion—we grieved over the loss of one baby, while we rejoiced in holding the other. It amazed me that I could feel such intense happiness and profound heartache, all at the same time.

A few days later, feelings of earthly sorrow and eternal joy permeated the small funeral service we held for Emily.

We gathered at a small cemetery in Blackfoot, Idaho, across the street from Mark's childhood home. We heard the wind whistle through the spruce tree that stood majestically over-looking the spot where Emily's body would lay. As the biting wind and snow continued to blow over the now barren potato fields nearby, we wrapped our coats more tightly around us. Even through the bitter cold, we felt a peaceful feeling as our extended family, including a handful of Emily's young cousins, gathered around and listened while Mark offered gratitude for their love and support. He expressed his appreciation for the principle of eternal families. I looked around at our little nieces and nephews who would never know their cousin on this earth.

Then, gazing into the older faces, many lined with years of living through good times as well as bad, I saw a quiet understanding that I would come to value more completely as the years went by.

There was one other feeling of gratitude that was very distinctive to me that day. Emily's body only took up half of the burial plot. How grateful I was that we didn't need the other half, and I even felt sorrow for the other family member who would need it someday, if at all. I was glad my "turn" was over. Years later, I was glad I could not have seen into the future.

> *Harmful habits are easy to fall into, particularly when we are feeling most vulnerable.*

As we lowered Emily's tiny casket into the ground, I had feelings that surprised me. I knew that her spirit was no longer in that little body, and yet I still recognized it as a beautiful masterpiece that Mark and I, with the help of God, had created. It was as if I had spent *months* shaping a beautiful work of art, only to bury it, where no one could enjoy it. It felt devastating.

Once we returned home, life continued. Since Amy needed to eat every two hours for the first few months of her life, and I was nursing her, I got very little sleep. Mark helped me when he could, giving her supplemental formula. We both hoped he could get the study time he needed to keep up his grades. Nicholas was a very active toddler, who had spent the previous few months with extended family members and was trying to grasp the reality of the situation. It was a very challenging time. Our devoted mothers and other family members came to help us. One day my little sister visited and simply brushed and styled my hair. It felt so good to be pampered a little, especially when I felt so physically and emotionally drained.

Life proved both painful and sweet at that time. Amy weighed only four and a half pounds, and looked even smaller than a Cabbage Patch doll. I found great joy in caring for her and watching Nicholas take over the role of the protective big brother. He called her "Toots." One day, when Amy was only a few months old, we were outside visiting with a neighbor and her children on the steps of our apartment complex. Nicholas decided he would take Amy, who was asleep in her stroller, on a walk around the quiet block where we lived. When I looked over and noticed the stroller and Nicholas gone, I felt a little panic, even though I had an idea of where they might be. I ran down the street and saw them as they turned the corner. He was marching along, singing to her as he went. My pounding heart warmed to see the love he had for his baby sister, but I couldn't help feeling the pain of not having Emily there to enjoy growing up with them.

Although the ache that comes from losing a child never really goes away, it does lessen over the years. Some parents even say that the pain is still as intense, but they learn to cope with the loss. As I have talked and agreed with other mothers who have lost children, I realize that thoughts of these little ones are there every day. The tears come and go, life goes on, happiness returns and joy can be found, and all the while, these children remain ever-present in our hearts.

Many times, though, they seem to be forgotten by the rest of the world. One Christmas season, about ten years after the twins' births, I had an experience that was especially meaningful and one I will never forget. It was the day after Thanksgiving, the so-called busiest shopping day of the year. I happened to be in a very crowded department store when I saw Carolyn Stone. She was one of the nurses who had taken care of Emily during the trip to Primary Children's Hospital in Salt Lake. Outside the members of my own family, Carolyn was the only other person on earth who had spent substantial time with our daughter. I recognized her from the picture we had taken and kept in Emily's baby book. In the photo, she stood by Emily's side, holding a small oxygen tube, which she removed long enough for the picture to be taken. I asked her if by chance she remembered Emily. I knew it was an unfair question; after all, working in the NICU, she had dealt with hundreds of babies. How could she remember our child? A smile came across her face as she told me that yes, she did remember. Carolyn recalled the incredible snowfall that day, and she tenderly told me how Emily responded when she rubbed the back of her finger across our daughter's little cheek. Many babies with heart problems, she explained, were fussy and did not respond well when touched or cuddled. But Emily had cooed and turned toward her as she tried to calm her. Right there, in those busy aisles of that crowded store, as people scurried about with their holiday shopping, this sweet woman gave me one of the best gifts I have ever received. What a thrill it was to hear this small memory of my baby!

Emotional burdens can make any problem more difficult because they diminish our ability to think clearly or focus on a solution.

Through the months of grief after Emily's death, I found food to be comforting. Eating quickly turned into a coping mechanism. The bloated feeling that came after overindulging was quite unpleasant, but it did not keep me from overeating the next time.

Fatigue was a major factor, too. Even though we had a lot

of help, I still didn't sleep well for months. Mark assisted me in feeding Amy, but he was still in school, and I wanted to allow him all the sleep he could get. For me, there were many sleepless nights, not only as I got up every two hours to feed Amy, but quite often when I also awoke to check on her just to make sure she was still breathing, which I learned was a common thing to do for mothers who had recently lost a baby. Frequently I mistook fatigue for what I thought was hunger, since food immediately relieved my discomfort. When I should have been grabbing a nap or at least an apple or carrot stick, I reached instead for cookies or chocolate, which were in easy reach and provided a quick pick-me-up. Buying them at the store was a little like buying comfort, or so I thought. It was also easy to overeat during meals. At the time, washing and preparing fruits and vegetables seemed to take too long, especially with the physical and emotional demands I was feeling.

My grief was complicated by the profound happiness I felt at having a beautiful little baby, as well as a toddler, at my side. The roller coaster of emotions continued. While I held Amy, I felt such joy to have her as well as her brother; then I would feel intense sadness as I missed Emily, then I would feel guilty over that sadness. I knew Amy would be a continuous reminder of Emily, as well as a constant comfort to me.

One day, when Amy was a few months old, I expressed concern to our pediatrician because she often cried, even though I had just fed her, burped her, changed her diaper, and could see she had every reason to be comfortable. The doctor saw no medical problem, but he pointed out the sense of loss that this tiny infant was experiencing. I ached inside when she cried, wondering if she were missing her twin. It was quite painful. We comforted each other. And we grieved together.

As the months passed, I was able to get more sleep, which helped tremendously, and I felt much better. However, the poor eating habits and lack of regular exercise remained with me, and I found my new lifestyle quite easy to live with.

The more I ate, the less I wanted to exercise, and the more weight I gained, the more I felt myself getting out of control. I was caught in the vicious cycle of eating to make myself feel better because of any emotion I experienced—sadness, disappointment, anxiety, or fatigue. I even ate when there was a reason to celebrate. I was well aware that there were many positive elements about my life, and eating was definitely part of enjoying those good times, too. However, I was soon feeling horrible about my weight—I felt unhealthy, and I knew I didn't look very healthy, either. So I would eat to feel better.

I was shocked as I saw pictures of myself that we took as Nicholas and Amy grew. What had happened to me? Was this really *my* body? I hardly recognized myself anymore. I realized I was looking less and less in mirrors as I passed by them, even trying to avoid them altogether. I spent less time getting ready in the mornings, and since my pretty clothes didn't fit well, I found comfort wearing large sweats and oversized T-shirts. I felt and looked sloppy.

I was beginning a journey in which I would struggle for many years to find a way back. My own, self-inflicted prison would be a place where I would spend more than a decade, not only wondering how I could escape, but if there were even a way out.

I was jarred back to my present situation. The bus had finally stopped. We were at the starting line.

CHAPTER TWO

Two Earthly Angels

It was almost 4:30 A.M., a half hour until race time. We grabbed our sweatshirts and Gatorade and got off the bus, wishing our fellow runners, our newfound friends, good luck. The parking lot, lit up by huge floodlights, illuminated small groups of runners. I overheard them laughing and sharing running stories. Some were trying to stay warm by jogging back and forth, and others were napping, right there on the ground, using their sweatshirts as pillows. Many were stretching, and others were meditating or listening to their headphones. Mark and I sat down and stretched.

A race official soon informed us that the wheelchair event would be starting. A handful of athletes rolled up to the starting line. Their bulging arm muscles were impressive. The bang of the gun echoed through the canyon, and off they rode into the darkness. I thought about the mountains that they would have to climb. It was inspiring to consider how they faced—and overcame—obstacles every day.

I realized how much I had taken my health for granted. I hoped I wouldn't be guilty of that after what I had been through the past year and a half. Watching these incredible athletes also made me think of the physical challenges affecting our daughters Sarah and Hillary. Eleven-year-old Sarah had struggled almost every day of her whole life. They were years full of pain, countless visits to the doctor, uncertainty, as well as hope.

Hillary, who was four, had been diagnosed with a very rare bone disease. There was still much uncertainty in her future.

Mark and I were learning a great deal as we traveled the rocky path with them. And we weren't out of the woods yet.

Nicholas was four and Amy was almost two when Sarah was born. They were thrilled to have a new little sister. After Mark completed his graduate work, we moved to Michigan, where Mark had a wonderful job working at Ford Motor Company. Although he enjoyed many aspects of his work, he continued to have a desire to earn a Ph.D and teach at a university. We often talked about his dream, and, as difficult as it was to imagine plunging back into more schooling, we worked toward that goal. Two years later, we moved to Texas, where we began four long yet rewarding years as Mark pursued a doctorate degree at Texas A&M. Living in Bryan/College Station, we were hundreds of miles from family and didn't know a soul when we first moved there. However, we soon found lifelong friends at our church and throughout the community. We relied on them as we headed into a most difficult time.

Sarah was now almost two years old, and was a very cheerful little girl. She had learned to walk at an early age, and loved to walk or run everywhere she went. That all changed just before her second birthday. She began favoring her right foot, and as the weeks passed, her limp continued to be more pronounced. Although she did not complain very much, there were times when we could easily see she was in pain. Something was definitely wrong. Friends began asking what she had done to her leg. I could not recall any specific time she had hurt herself, and I wondered if she wasn't just experiencing growing pains. However, a few weeks later, when I lifted her out of her car seat and placed her gently on the ground, she screamed in so much pain she could not even walk for a few minutes. Frightened, I called the pediatrician. The excruciating pain had subsided, but the limp was now worse than ever. The doctor could see that there was a problem, but he could not detect exactly what was wrong. He too suspected growing pains. "Keep an eye on her," he said.

The tenderness was concentrated in her right foot, which she held very rigidly. She also could not point her toes. The pain and limp continued to worsen over the next few weeks. One night, while she was sleeping, I tenderly tried straightening her foot, thinking her muscles might just be stiff. She immediately woke up and winced with pain. That little foot just did not seem to be able to move. Frustrated, I took her back to the doctor.

He suggested we see an orthopedic specialist. Because her condition was not life threatening, it was weeks before we could get in to see him. Meanwhile, little Sarah's pain continued. It was worse when she first woke up in the morning and after her nap, as well as after she had been sitting in her car seat or highchair. She also tired more easily than she had before. When we finally got in to see the bone specialist, he took some X rays and, not finding anything wrong, he suspected there might be a hairline fracture. He put her in a cute little cast for a few weeks. Sarah thought it was rather amusing walking and running around in her cast, and although there was no improvement, the cast held her ankle rigid, which seemed to alleviate some of the pain.

Our next visit was to a neurologist. Once again, we had to wait many weeks to get in, with Sarah's pain continuing to affect her daily. My frustration and distress were mounting. I felt helpless, and watching her struggle just to walk was painful for me as well. The doctor did more tests, including MRIs, where he could examine her spinal cord and her brain. He concluded, "I can see there is something wrong, but I can't find any neurological problem." We were grateful to hear that, but we wondered where to turn next.

It became increasingly difficult for me to focus on much else but trying to alleviate Sarah's pain, while trying to figure out what else we might do for her. I was not concerned about taking very good care of myself because I was trying so hard to care for Sarah, as well as our two older children. With Mark so busy with school, I was tutoring to help make ends meet. Money was tight and stress was high.

Mark and I had many discussions about Sarah's health. Early on, he had given her a father's blessing, and he had felt inspired to promise her that she would outgrow this vicious malady. I continued to cling to that promise, trying to remember that my own timetable was possibly quite different from that of the Lord's. I wanted her to be healed *now!* Mark's unwavering faith was very reassuring and helped me cope with the frustration and helplessness that accompanied the months of uncertainty and watching Sarah suffer. I knew I needed to further develop my faith and trust my Father in Heaven. I sent pleas heavenward more often, and I felt determined to discover the cause of the misery that was robbing Sarah of a normal childhood. Her condition was now affecting everything we did as a family. Anytime we wanted to go on even a small outing, we had to plan accordingly, since she could not walk very far. We often used her stroller, but she encountered so much pain even sitting that frequently we had to return home. I gave her Tylenol and other pain relievers, but they did little to help.

We visited more doctors. One specialist ordered a custom-made leg brace. I was anxious to see if this would help. After a few weeks, he checked her again. He decided that it had not been on long enough to see any improvement, so he advised her to wear it a few more months. It did not seem to be helping at all, other than maintaining her ankle in an unbending position, which alleviated a small amount of the pain.

During one Christmas we spent in Utah, Sarah's pain became so severe that we took her to the emergency room, where they performed a bone scan. The doctors who examined her could see there was a problem but could not determine what it was. I had been hoping they could see it from a new angle. Nothing was detected, however. I cried with helplessness. My little girl could barely walk, and I couldn't believe that through all the advancements of modern medicine, no one could give us an answer. All I could do was try to ease her suffering.

Almost eighteen long months passed as we continued to seek new opinions. One specialist was very blunt. He said, "She has a condition called tarsal coalition. You will just have to accept the fact, Mrs. Hansen, that she will never lead a normal life. That foot will always be rigid; she will never dance or play sports or do anything else where she will have to use her ankles for support." He seemed so sure of himself; however, I refused to accept his diagnosis. I continued to reflect on the father's blessing Sarah had received, as well as my own gut feeling that we would eventually find an answer. I just wished we knew where to find the solution. Was it not to be in this life? Would Sarah carry this burden her entire earthly existence?

Our concerns, as well as the medical bills, were mounting. Sarah continued wanting to be very active, and loved to run around with Nicholas and Amy, but she was also in pain most of the time. She expressed this soreness by limping and telling us her foot hurt, although she desperately did not want to let it slow her down. She discovered, however, that her leg hurt a lot less if she did not move it as much. It was heartbreaking to see how badly she wanted to run and play hard, but because of the pain how she was forced to limit herself. By this time, there was a remarkable difference in her feet. Her right foot behaved like a clubfoot. She continued to hold it very rigid, and could not seem to straighten it. There was also swelling in her ankle.

We cannot let a sense of helplessness become paralyzing. Maintaining hope and continuing to search for answers, as difficult and uncomfortable as it may be, is crucial.

I was now pregnant again. I had continued to gain weight and was heavier than ever. Even so, I was thrilled to be having another baby. This prospect brought such a ray of sunshine into our lives! I was nauseated, as I had been the other times, but I was looking forward to another little one joining our family.

Each night, as I leaned over to kiss each child good night, they would kiss my stomach, so excited about the arrival of a new sibling. The prenatal tests all looked promising. We felt very fortunate thinking about this healthy baby.

We were glad to have this birth to look forward to because dealing with Sarah's condition was heart-wrenching, and I felt increasingly helpless to provide her any relief. Certainly the Texas heat, the stress of being in school, and the extra hormones of pregnancy didn't help. I was grateful for concerned friends and family, but I also just wanted someone to tell us what to do about Sarah and where to turn for answers. I wanted that crystal ball. She had seen numerous doctors who had offered differing opinions, and our heads were spinning. We continued researching many different doctors throughout Texas. We asked friends, acquaintances, and those who worked in the medical field who they thought we should see. Our search led us to an orthopedic specialist in a large city just over one hundred miles from our home. He was supposed to be "the best of the best" in the entire South. I set up an appointment for Sarah to get in as quickly as we could, which was still months away. I was hopeful and anxious that he would *at last* be able to identify the problem.

The day finally came. Sarah and I traveled two hours to his office, and came armed with reports, scans, X rays, and lab results. I mentioned to him that from what we had learned, he was very well respected, and his reputation spoke volumes. He smiled a bit haughtily and seemed well aware of his status. He glanced through the reports and then performed the exam. He opted to do a bone scan, so we were there most of the day.

Late that afternoon, we sat in the waiting room while he

finished analyzing his findings. Sarah, still sleepy from the seda-
tion, lay drowsily in my arms, and the time passed very slowly. I
looked around at all the other patients. None of them seemed
particularly thrilled to be there, and I wondered how much their
ailments had affected their lives. With each long minute that
passed, I continued to pray and hope that this specialist would
have the answer.

I looked down at little slumbering Sarah, now three and a
half years old. She had experienced so much pain throughout
much of her young life. I still felt incredibly helpless, but I was
also hopeful that we would soon find a solution.

After what seemed like hours, the doctor came strolling into
the waiting room. He walked over and sat down beside me.
There was an unmistakable arrogance in his manner. In a voice
loud enough for the other patients and parents to hear, he said,
"Mrs. Hansen, there is absolutely nothing wrong with your
child. There have been more than enough tests performed,
including those we have done here today. We have not found
any problem. There is nothing wrong with her! Take her home,
quit babying her, make her get up and walk, even when she
doesn't want to, and be firm with her!"

And with that, he got up and briskly walked back to his
office. I sat there, frozen. That was *it*? This was his explanation?
For months, I had been waiting to see this man and had
invested so much hope that he would be the one to finally find
the problem. Tears welled up in my weary eyes. I looked around
at the people, many of them staring at me, and I couldn't even
register a response. This seemed like a bad dream. I had felt so
optimistic! His words that there was nothing wrong and his
implication that I had been babying her for the last eighteen
months left me reeling. I just sat there, unmoving, while at the

same time I could hardly wait to get out of there. I was devastated by his pompous and calloused approach; I had not even been able to utter a word of response to him. I did not even feel a sense of embarrassment at having a whole waiting room full of people witness his heartless speech. Nobody offered to help, and I couldn't bring myself to ask for it. With tears tumbling down my face, I gathered Sarah in my arms, and, with a heavy heart and very pregnant belly, I trudged to the car.

I had been certain this doctor would be able to find the problem. Instead, he had not even offered a sliver of sympathy or encouragement. Traveling this long, arduous road, we had come to a dead end. For an agonizing year and a half, we had seen doctor after doctor, hearing different opinions. We had explored every avenue we could think of. What should we do now? Whether it was parental intuition or just knowing Sarah so well, Mark and I both knew that there was *something* wrong. We strongly felt that Sarah was not capable of the lazy behavior this doctor thought she was exhibiting. She was three years old! She *wanted* to be out running and playing. That doctor had accused me of *babying* her! I knew I was not the perfect mother, but Mark and I certainly were not guilty of doing that with this child.

While Sarah continued to sleep during the long, two-hour drive home through the wide open Texas plain, a million thoughts ran through my head. As I looked around, I noticed that there were enough ranches and roaming cattle along this stretch of road to make a decent John Wayne movie. I rubbed my belly as I felt the baby kick, knowing he was unaware of what his mother and big sister were experiencing. My thoughts drifted away from Sarah, my main concern at the moment, to wondering if my weight had anything to do with how this doctor had treated us. Would he have seen things differently, shown more compassion or exhibited a kinder bedside manner if I had not been so overweight? I honestly could not help but speculate. It made me sick inside to think of the possibility of my weight having anything to do with how my children were treated, medically or otherwise. I could not help but think he would have been much less judgmental and insensitive if I had not been so heavy. I reached for another Tootsie Roll.

Stephen Mark was born just a few months later. The pregnancy, although uncomfortable, especially in my now quite overweight body, had been tolerable. He was healthy, and I had not had any complications, other than the incredible stress I felt about Sarah's physical health and a feeling of utter helplessness about it all. Although little Sarah was disappointed we didn't name him "Barney," her favorite purple dinosaur and the last name of a good friend as well as a revered colleague of Mark's, we were all grateful for the happiness Stephen brought into our lives. I vowed, as I had with every other pregnancy, to "lose weight" and enjoy life as a fit and healthy mother. However, my main concern continued to be for Sarah. We still did not know what was ailing her.

A few months later, we journeyed to Utah for my youngest sister's wedding. During the wedding reception, I noticed my mother's cousin, with her husband, Dale G. Johnson, M.D., who was Chief of Surgery at Primary Children's Hospital. I knew he was probably asked medical questions wherever he went. I felt a little uncomfortable asking him to examine Sarah right there at a crowded social gathering, but at that point I was desperate to try anything. Dale smiled and kindly said he would be glad to look at her foot. As I pulled off Sarah's frilly white sock, I realized that mothers will do anything, including risk

35

embarrassment, to help their children. I was also grateful for his kindhearted concern. I briefly told him the events of the past year and a half. He examined her swollen and immobile ankle. He immediately suspected arthritis. I thought I had heard him wrong. Wasn't arthritis a "grandparent's disease"? Certainly, it did not affect children! I had never heard of that before. He explained a little about Juvenile Rheumatoid Arthritis. The stiffness and inflammation that is present causes redness, swelling, heat, and soreness in the joints. As he spoke, I considered her symptoms. It all seemed to make sense. It seemed to also affect her left knee as well as her right ankle. He said she should see a pediatric rheumatologist as soon as possible. He promised he would help us find one in Texas.

Within a few days, we had an appointment set up with a doctor in Houston who would see her as soon as we returned home. While we awaited a confirmation, we felt like the sun was finally coming out from behind the dark clouds that had long ago worn out their welcome. There had been countless times we had felt hope at finding a resolution, only to have it dashed; but this time, we felt different. We felt a kind of peace.

We were soon at the Texas Children's Medical Center in Houston, in the office of Barry Myones, M.D. He was very kind and sympathetic, and Sarah liked his beard. He performed lab work and examined her very thoroughly and soon confirmed that she had Pauciarticular Juvenile Rheumatoid Arthritis. Although we were not delighted our daughter had this potentially crippling disease, we felt a huge relief to finally understand what had been attacking her little body for so long. Dr. Myones prescribed medication and physical therapy. Her condition improved, even within a few weeks. We were elated! We were advised, however, that there would likely be tough times ahead.

We learned that Juvenile Rheumatoid Arthritis, or JRA, involves abnormalities of the immune system. There was still uncertainty about the severity of the disease or the course it would take.

Stephen was now a few months old. With four young children to care for and Mark working hard in school, I had little time for myself. But I did not mind; we were relieved to have identified the problem and to be doing something that we knew would help Sarah. She enjoyed getting in the whirlpool bath and playing with the "toys" at physical therapy. Since she was going every other day, we soon became good friends

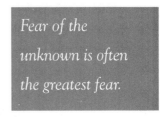

Fear of the unknown is often the greatest fear.

with the therapists. One day, while sitting in church, a member gave a heartfelt talk on how therapy had helped him work out some problems. Sarah heard some of his words and turned to me very excited. She said, rather loudly and joyously, "Hey, Mom! That guy goes to therapy, just like we do!"

Over the next few years, the children and I took many trips to see Dr. Myones in Houston. Since it was a long drive, we often visited the zoo or other places while we were there. We tried to make it a fun excursion for everyone. Sarah's care continued to take a huge chunk of my time and energy. I learned how chronic illness affects family dynamics. Often, parents are so understandably caught up in the physical and emotional care of the afflicted child that the needs of the other siblings frequently fall by the wayside. It can be an extremely demanding and difficult circumstance for parents.

In trying to juggle Sarah's needs, as well as those of my other children, I continued to put my own needs on the back burner. Actually, I think somewhere along the line, I shoved them right off the stove. Mark was hard at work on his dissertation. I was fortunate to find a part-time job teaching English as a second language, and we were able to arrange our time so we did not need to find a baby-sitter. Although I loved teaching and enjoyed using my rusty Spanish, I did not feel I was setting aside enough time to properly care for myself. Our lives were no different than those of other young families; they revolved around work, school, meals, laundry, a few soccer games, helping out at the children's school, Scout activities, serving in church responsibilities, more laundry, doctor visits, and quite often, searching out ways to keep cool in the scorching Texas heat. Years later, I would realize how much better off I would have been, especially in those critical times of caring for Sarah, if I had also better cared for Sarah's mother.

The next ten years were not easy for our daughter. She endured innumerable visits to the doctor, tests, injections, medication, pain, and stiffness. When Sarah was five, we moved back to Utah. Mark had finished his schooling and had accepted a position teaching in the Business School at BYU. Although hesitant to be in over our heads trying to care for Sarah's needs as well as those of our three other children, we did want to have at least one more child. We were thrilled when baby Hillary came along a year after our move.

Sarah's care continued at Primary Children's Hospital, where we found wonderful doctors and nurses. She continued to need weekly injections of methotrexate to treat the inflammation. We found ways of making the process as easy as possible. Ginger, a wonderful friend and neighbor, worked as a nurse at a nearby hospital. Her daughter was one of Sarah's best friends, and all four of us would gather each Sunday evening at the "nursing station," which was the counter in Ginger's comfy kitchen. We would attempt to distract Sarah from the prick of the needle and the sting of the medication, while Ginger carefully and gently administered the injection. Each week, as Sarah lifted up her sleeve, I offered a silent prayer that it would not be too painful, that the medication would do what it was supposed to do and not adversely affect her, and also offered thanks for our angel Ginger.

The arthritis, which attacked Sarah's joints, was also capable of manifesting itself in her eyes. It was rare, but possible. So, along with her rheumatologist, we saw a pediatric ophthalmologist who specialized in doing the kind of exam that detected this condition. Sarah was examined every three months, and each time her eyes were given a clean bill of health. After a few years, I even wondered about the need to continue these eye exams. However, I am glad I continued taking her to be checked.

At one point, Sarah was experiencing a particularly painful flare-up. We were at the ophthalmologist's office once again, but this time he was spending a longer time than he usually did examining her left eye. "Hmmmmm," was all he said. My heart started to pound.

"Hmmmmm," he said again. He flipped on the light switch and moved the machine away from Sarah's face. He turned to me and somberly explained that there was inflammation, or uveitis, present in her left eye. He went on to say that she would need to have steroid drops, and this would need to be carefully controlled or she could lose her sight. I went numb.

A few days later, a second eye specialist confirmed Sarah's condition. Over the next few months, as we tried to regulate the amount of steroids she needed, we made weekly visits to the eye doctor. That time was particularly stressful. We were now quite concerned about Sarah's eyes, as well as her joints, which continued to be affected. For many weeks, I was putting drops into Sarah's eye each hour—which meant spending a good deal of time at the school. I did not want to leave this critical task to an already overworked school nurse or teacher. By this time, Stephen was four years old and Hillary had just turned one. I dragged them along back and forth to the school, and in a short time, everyone seemed to know them by name. Some days, it was simply easier to keep Sarah home. We continued to work to regulate the amount of drops she needed, and monitor potential side effects. Finally, she went from having the drops every hour to having them every two hours, every four, then three times a day, twice a day, and finally once a day. We were eventually able to wean her off the drops entirely, although a flare-up usually meant more eye inflammation and more eye drops. It was challenging staying on top of the disease.

When Sarah was first diagnosed with arthritis, even though we were relieved to finally know of her condition, we felt somewhat alarmed and unaware of all the implications. As we educated ourselves about the nature of the disease and became more familiar with her treatment, and how to help her manage, we felt more at peace. Still, there were many times I would just hold her and yearn to make it all better. As I knew other mothers would do if they could, I wished that I could take on her pain and discomfort myself.

Then, in the midst of one of Sarah's worst flare-ups, Mark noticed lumps on the fingers of Hillary's right hand. When he showed them to me and asked me if I was aware of them, I shook my head. My first thought was that she had somehow broken her fingers and they had failed to heal correctly. How could we have missed that? Hillary was a typical two-year-old, into everything. What had happened? Her hand did not seem to hurt her, but if her fingers had indeed broken recently, why hadn't we been aware of it? Then a disturbing thought turned my stomach. Did she have arthritis, too? Sarah was eight years old at the time, and I could not imagine little Hillary experiencing all that Sarah was currently suffering.

We took Hillary to our pediatrician, who immediately sent her for X rays. The results were astonishing; she appeared to have a very rare disease called Ollier's Disease, or Multiple Enchondromatosis. Hillary had tumors growing inside the bones of her right hand. Although it was late on a Friday afternoon, our doctor, who had never seen a case like this before, went right to work doing research to help us all understand the disease a little more. What we found were horrifying pictures and information about this serious and potentially disfiguring disease.

We went again to Primary Children's Hospital, where a pediatric orthopedic surgeon, who specialized in tumors, examined her. Hillary had also been born with multiple hemangiomas, which were raised red splotches we had affectionately called "angel kisses." Many people have hemangiomas on various parts of their bodies. However, those, together with the now present bone tumors, suggested that Hillary might have an even rarer condition called Maffucci's Syndrome, which was very similar to Ollier's but potentially even more serious. The doctor said that only time and examinations would tell which condition she had. He also said that there were only a few other cases like this in the entire Intermountain West.

I felt dizzy as we left his office. We had no idea what to expect or how severely this disease would affect her. I wondered how in the world these things could be happening to our children, and once again, I felt incredibly helpless.

I e-mailed a few other parents whose children had Ollier's, and even visited with one mother on the phone. She was very candid and told me about her daughter and the multiple surgeries she'd had, which included having tumors removed, bones rebuilt, as well as having her leg and arm bones lengthened. To say the least, it was all rather frightening.

This mother, who had started a support group for others with this condition, mailed me additional information. The day it arrived, I eagerly tore open the large envelope, which was full of data she had gathered from physicians and families coping with this disease. Included in the various papers was a message from "Make a Wish," the wonderful foundation that grants the desires of children with—wait a minute—of children with *fatal conditions.* Why were *they* sending me information? It all started to sink in. I was horrified.

We divulged Hillary's condition to our family and to a few friends. We still wanted to find out more about it as well as its severity before we revealed too much, and I didn't feel like talking about it. When others kindly asked us how we were doing, "Fine," was the answer we gave. But inside, I was screaming. "No! I'm *not* fine! I don't understand! This *can't* be happening! What are we doing wrong? Why do our children have these problems?" I asked myself these questions repeatedly. The agony I felt came from not knowing just how this disease would affect Hillary, and from my sense of utter helplessness. The cases and implications we had read about were shocking.

Mark and I were in disbelief. Sarah was in the middle of an arthritis flare-up and was so stiff and sore that she had missed many days of school. We had lost Emily from a heart defect, and now another challenge faced us. It seemed strange that so many physical problems were occurring in our children.

During this time we prayed often for strength and understanding. We discovered that as our prayers became more frequent, we developed more faith, and had a stronger desire to live in such a way to ensure that our heartfelt pleas would be heard. Even through our fear and confusion, we felt a divine calming influence. Mark gave Hillary a father's blessing. As he spoke of how she would cope with this disease, I wanted to stop him, right there, in the middle of the beautiful blessing, and ask him to just pronounce her "healed." I wanted so badly for that to happen! Once again, it was not to be.

> *Viewed in perspective, challenges can help us appreciate our blessings.*

Our faith would continue to be tested. I wondered if we were just extremely slow learners. We sensed that Hillary's condition would not necessarily just go away, but that we would be made equal to the task of caring for her, and that she would come out of this all right, regardless of the severity. What a wonderful, peaceful feeling that was. In time, the calm feeling that encompassed my heart overtook and far surpassed my own craving for an immediate miracle.

However, even through the peace that I felt, there were still many unknowns. What course would this disease take? How severe would it be? We knew there was not yet a cure. The case studies we had learned about were alarming. The helpless feeling I had felt so often was manifest yet again. And, once more, food seemed so soothing. I often felt like drowning my sorrows in a big lake of chocolate.

I also wanted to be proactive in educating myself about this disease. I went up to the Medical Library at the University of Utah, in Salt Lake City, looking for the latest research. Because this condition is so rare, there is still much that is unknown. The uncertainty is one of the most difficult things to face, but Mark and I have both remarked how dealing with this challenge has helped us to appreciate her as well as our other children even more. We cherish every day that we have with her.

Meanwhile, pounds and inches kept adding up. Although prayer played an important part in my life, I continued to cope principally by turning to food. Having these babies had taken a physical toll on my body. Coping with Emily's death and facing Sarah and Hillary's problems took an even greater toll on me emotionally. By the autumn of 2000, I weighed an all-time high, and emotionally I was close to my all-time low.

Those two distances were about to become even further apart.

This early morning adventure continued to be a time of reflection on this difficult yet amazing journey. I felt humbled to be the mother of these children who were so willing to accept the challenges of life without question or complaint. I also felt unequal to be among these incredible runners. They all looked so athletic and prepared. Was I truly ready to run this marathon? I had done so much preparation for this day, studying books and plowing through months of training runs that had taken an incredible amount of time and energy. Some of those runs had been wonderful experiences; others had left me questioning my attempt. However, they had all been exhilarating. I looked around again at the other runners. They came in all ages and sizes. Some donned expensive running clothes, but most just wore shorts and T-shirts. As I watched them, I realized each one

of them had a story. I knew they had also made a tremendous effort to be there. We would all soon discover just how effectively we had trained. There had been days when I just did not feel like running, when I would have given almost anything for someone else to go on my run for me. However, I came to understand that in training to run a race, there is no one who can do the work for the runner. Physically, I alone had to complete the often-grueling training. But doing so helped me to more fully realize the simple yet difficult truth—that as nice as it would be to avoid life's tough situations, such as I experienced with Emily's death and facing the health challenges of our daughters, I came to better understand that no one else can undergo those struggles for us. The wheelchair athletes certainly understood that concept. They also realized what I now more fully comprehended, that although plenty of help is available, we need to be willing to face our trials and find the strength to deal with them effectively. And it *can* be done!

CHAPTER THREE

An Angel Son

The time of pondering and being amazed by all these incredible athletes was over. It was time to line up, get our watches set, and listen for the starting gun. I wondered if I could run and hide in the porta-potties, or even fit into the plastic bag that held my sweatshirt, which I threw, along with all the other bags full of runner's belongings, onto the truck that was headed down the mountain to the finish line. No, I knew *that* was impossible—there was no way out at this point. It wasn't like anyone was forcing me to do this, but I did wonder for a moment or two if I was really ready to run 26.2 miles that morning. There was no doubt about my desire, but I also thought about the horror stories of runners getting dehydrated halfway through the race and having to quit, or collapsing with a heart attack just before the finish line. I quickly shoved those thoughts out of my mind as I continued to think about my own journey.

When I was thirty-nine years old, I was horrified to realize I weighed one hundred pounds more than when I got married. That is a small, but entire person! I wondered if my dear husband recognized that. He was a smart man. Certainly smart enough to know how much weight I had gained, and even smarter and kinder than to belittle or criticize me about it. Sure, we occasionally discussed how we wanted to enjoy a healthier lifestyle. Nevertheless, I often felt helpless to actually do anything about it and then felt disgusted with myself because I knew I *could* help it. I often felt imprisoned in my huge body, screaming to escape its mighty clutch. It was as if someone had locked me in a cell and told me the key was in there *somewhere*, if only I could find it and break free. For over thirteen years, I struggled to find that key. There were times when I wondered if such a key really existed. I was hoping, deep down, that it *was* possible, but I was unable, time and time again, to make it happen.

Realizing that there are some things in life over which we have no control can be difficult, but accepting that concept is fundamental in dealing with challenges.

I tried. Boy, did I try. I attempted about every diet and idea that wasn't too outlandish. I educated myself about proper nutrition, I took "Slim for Life" classes, I drank meal replacement drinks, I listened to tapes on weight-loss, I tried over-the-counter diet pills, I tried lo-carb, no-carb, hi-protein plans, I got a gym membership, I bought books and meal-planning guides, all in attempts to improve my health. Nothing seemed to work.

I also walked and occasionally rode my bike. However, I only seemed to make time for exercise when I could fit it in, after I had taken care of everyone else's needs. Taking care of myself was way at the bottom of my priority list. I deserved a little credit, however. After all, I was helping to raise a young family, and I loved being a wife and mother. Our children, especially Sarah and Hillary and their health issues, required time and attention.

Over the years, as I got bigger and bigger, I made the same resolution every New Year's Eve—"Lose Weight." There it was, always right at the top of my list, year after year. I would write down ideas on how I thought I was going to accomplish it *this* year: a new exercise plan, some new diet, a renewed confidence that this year I was *really* going to do it. Over the years, I tried to become creative with this particular goal. I would write it down. I would type it and post it where I could see it often. I would make "goal charts." For a few days, even weeks, I seemed to do okay. Although I had good intentions, I just could not seem to stick with it. I would experience a disappointment or have a discouraging day, and there I would be, right back to my old eating habits. I cannot even begin to count how many times I fell and would start to pick myself back up, only to experience more failure. I would end up more discouraged and disgusted with myself. I did shed pounds of tears over the years, as I hated my body and felt like a miserable failure. Then I would eat in an attempt to feel better, only to feel guilty and frustrated afterwards. Once again, I would turn to food for comfort. The vicious cycle continued, year after painful year. And I couldn't get out.

It was December 31, 2000. It had been almost thirteen years since Emily's death. I was making my usual resolution to lose weight. This time, though, after so many years of living with obesity and feeling out of control, I gave up trying to make it a goal. It seemed useless. No matter how hard I tried, I just could not do it. As I had many other nights, I thought during that evening that I may as well face up to the fact that I would be fat forever. Why not have fun along the way?

I was also pregnant. Even though I was thrilled to be having another baby, the pregnancy had come as somewhat of a surprise. I was very apprehensive because of wanting to be able to effectively care for Sarah and Hillary. I also did not want to lose another baby. And I was concerned that even when I wasn't carrying a baby, I felt and looked nine months pregnant. Although I knew that trying to lose weight during pregnancy was not a good idea, I certainly did not want to gain any more weight than would be healthy for the baby.

> We need to keep focusing forward. It may take as much energy to go backward as it does to keep moving ahead.

Therefore, for the first time, I made a conscious decision *not* to have "Lose Weight" as one of my goals for that next year. Although it was still a dream, it now seemed absolutely unattainable. It appeared as if I were giving up.

Because of complications in my previous pregnancies, especially the twins, my doctor performed an ultrasound. He discovered what he thought might be another set of multiples. I was not sure whether to be elated or alarmed. I felt a little of both. During the next few weeks, I had a few more ultrasounds, where we discovered one of the babies had stopped growing. What had appeared to be a second baby was now dissolving. Because it was still early in the pregnancy, the emotional impact was not quite as high as it might have been later on. Although I felt badly about missing another possibility of having two babies, I was relieved to learn that the other baby appeared healthy.

I was so excited for this baby's arrival. I was looking forward to feeling its soft little cheek against mine. I was especially looking forward to having older children around now to help care for the baby, and our children were excited to have another sibling in the family. I knew it was not going to be easy, but we could do it. I was delighted to be having another child.

On April 10, 2001, I went to the hospital to have another ultrasound and possibly an amniocentesis, since lab work indicated possible problems. Everything seemed fine, to me, however. I had felt the baby move and had suffered extreme nausea throughout the pregnancy, which for me was normal.

Because of having three children born with genetic problems, Mark and I first spoke with a genetics counselor that morning. He explained the results from the lab work and told us that after the ultrasound examination, the doctors would determine if more tests were needed. I felt calm.

We finished the consultation, even joking with the counselor about having to meet with him at all. We went to the examination room, where Mark helped me onto the table. I flinched as the cold ultrasound jelly came squirting out onto my big belly. I tried to recall just how many of these ultrasounds I'd had over the years. By now, even with my untrained eye, I knew what to look for. As the technician began, my first thought as I looked up at the screen was that something must be wrong with the machine. The baby, a little boy, was not moving. I wondered if there was just too much fat on my stomach to get a good picture. The technician moved the scanner around some more, and I could see a perfectly formed baby, including cute little arms and legs, as well as tiny hands and feet. All his little parts looked fine. They were just . . . still. The technician leaned closer to the screen as she narrowed in on the chest. His little heart was not beating.

Now I was *sure* the machine was broken. Why was it only taking still pictures? Surely this wasn't happening! No, it couldn't be. I had just felt him kicking the day before! The technician quickly left to find the radiologist. "Yes, go get the radiologist," I thought. *She* would fix the machine and show us that our baby was just fine.

But it was not to be. When the doctor came in and rolled the scanner around on my abdomen, we saw that the circumstances had not changed. "The heart is not beating," she said quietly. She showed us the evidence of our baby's condition, as she gently pointed out his motionless little heart. My own heart was pounding and felt as if once again, it would break, as our worst fears were confirmed. Our baby was dead.

I wanted to scream and wake up from this horrible, recurring nightmare. Mark was quiet as he helped me up from the table. The radiologist left us alone briefly while she stepped out to speak on the phone with my obstetrician. Amid the tears, the hurt and disbelief were evident in our eyes, as Mark and I just sat there looking at each other, not knowing what to say. We numbly listened as the radiologist came back and tenderly told us to go home, and as soon as we were ready that afternoon, we were to go to the neighboring hospital, where I would deliver the lifeless body of our precious baby.

We had arrived there that morning lighthearted and even joking with the medical staff. We now walked down the corridor in a daze. I loved and I hated that place. Nicholas, Amy, and Emily had all been born there. Nick's birth had been a completely happy occasion. Having little Amy had been joyous as well. But just down the hall was the room where Emily had taken her last breath. And we had just discovered here that our little boy was now gone, too.

Leaving the hospital, we saw people scurrying back and forth, taking care of business. We drove home, baffled and disheartened. Tearfully we picked up three-year-old Hillary from a friend's house where she had been playing, and we waited for our older children to come home from school. We were glad they all came right home, and we explained to them what was happening. We also called John Wadsworth, our church leader, and he came right over. Together we prayed, and John expressed his love and concern. More tears were shed as Mark and I left for the hospital.

Arriving twenty minutes later at the hospital, a kind nurse, aware of our situation, tried to hurry us down the "happy corridor," as it was called, past the rooms where all the laboring and delivering mothers were. We kept walking, around the corner, down another hall, into a room in the far corner. I noticed the recently posted, all-too-familiar sticker on the door, advising doctors and nurses that in this room there was a mother who would not be taking her baby home.

By 9:30 that evening, after one more thorough exam to confirm our baby's death, our sympathetic doctor started what I hoped would be an easy and quick delivery. But instead it proved difficult and painful.

The nurse smiled sadly as the doctor administered the drugs to begin the labor, and she gently encouraged me to get an epidural. I had experienced dizziness from having had one during the birth of our son, Stephen. I did not want to feel groggy or sleepy; I wanted to remember every minute of the short time we would have with our baby.

As the labor pains increased during the night, I thought twice about that epidural, through the four long hours of extremely painful contractions. I had experienced this sort of pain during childbirth before. However, this time, the anguish came with the knowledge that there was not going to be the usual happy ending, and that made it all even worse.

Little Eric finally arrived shortly after 2:00 in the morning, on April 11, 2001. His lifeless body looked so sweet and perfect. What could have gone wrong? (Lab work would later prove inconclusive.) His tiny parts were all there. I counted ten fingers and ten toes. I was amazed at how much love I already felt for this little person.

Faith and prayer provide comfort, understanding, and strength.

The doctor, though very skilled, seemed to have a difficult time getting the placenta to deliver. Sweat formed on his brow as he worked intensely to remove it. If the labor pains and birth of the baby were very painful, delivering the placenta was absolutely excruciating. My heart certainly did not want to give up this baby. It seemed now as if there was no part of me willing to let him go.

It was, at long last, completed. I was utterly exhausted. Physically, I still hurt considerably, but it was nothing compared to the emotional ache I felt. We spent some cherished time holding our tiny son. We took pictures of him, and although I knew I would have those pictures to look at over the years, I realized the images I captured with my memory of that moment would be the ones that would be most precious.

Later that morning, as I got in the car to go home, I looked up at the sky. It was a bright spring day. Yet, the deep blueness of the heavens did not seem to be as vibrant as it usually was on such a beautiful day. To me, it appeared dull and dreary.

Family members, neighbors, and friends stopped by with flowers, food, and gifts. Some simply gave us hugs. Mark and I took great comfort in the wonderful outpouring of love and support. Because baby caskets at the funeral home seemed so big for such a tiny body, our good friend and neighbor, who is also a master craftsman, made a casket for Eric. His wife lined it with white satin cloth, including a tiny pillow. We wrapped the little body in a lovely white blanket made by Mark's mother. It even had a tiny sash. We also covered him with another lovely blanket that my friend Lisa had made, with delicate tatting around the edges. She had so thoughtfully made *me* a pillowcase out of the same material. It covered a fluffy pillow "to hug on those nights when I was missing my babies." Another neighbor who owned a floral business made a lovely spray of tiny white roses for the top of the casket. We were so touched by the love expressed to us by our kind friends and family. It was humbling to think of all time and effort they had invested in such caring works of art that would be tucked away, not to be seen until perhaps eternity.

A few days later, on a chilly spring morning, we were once again at the peaceful country cemetery near Blackfoot, Idaho. Under the direction and with permission of the cemetery staff, Mark and our son Nicholas, as well as Mark's dad, brothers, and some of their sons, dug the grave, next to where we had buried Emily thirteen years earlier. It was quite a moving scene to watch these men digging together for their tiny relative. I sadly smiled when I remembered about having had my "turn" at losing a child. I never thought I would ever have to bury another baby.

Later that day, we held a short graveside service, where our family members gathered around as we expressed love for one another and for this little one who had already tenderly touched our hearts in such a big way. While Mark spoke of the gratitude we felt for our family, I looked around at our children. They were not perfect. They did not always do what we asked. Their rooms got messy. They would forget to put their clothes away. They procrastinated on school projects. Yet, now, none of that seemed to matter at all. I felt such an intense love for them that was stronger and deeper than anything I could even imagine.

> *We will not succeed if we quit trying. Just because we have failed countless times before is no reason to ever give up!*

After Mark's simple dedication of the grave, I wrapped my coat tighter around me while he and his dad lowered the small casket into the grave. It was a cool morning, but the sun was shining and several birds were happily chirping. A crisp wind blew, as it usually did in that part of the Snake River Valley. In the fields surrounding the cemetery, a few crops showed signs of life. The world seemed to be eagerly anticipating this fresh beginning. Springtime was breathing new life into the cold, desolate ground, just as my world seemed to be crashing down once again.

For days afterward, I felt physically and emotionally empty. I couldn't remember ever feeling such an actual hollowness as I did then. The void seemed to permeate my soul. Although Eric had never taken a breath, I had felt life from him, and I still ached for this child.

The feelings I experienced thirteen years earlier, with Emily's death, came flooding back. When she died, I also had her tiny twin, whom I was thrilled to have, as well as a toddler, who both needed me. I simply had to move on. This time, Hillary, the youngest of our five living children, was three and a half, with older siblings to help care for her. Although I was so grateful for my children and loving husband, my arms and heart still ached with emptiness. I was terribly disappointed and heartbroken.

One thought that echoed in my mind was that there are some things in life over which we have no control. As far as I knew, there had been nothing I had done or not done to cause the deaths of my children. Other than having an overweight body, I tried carefully to create a healthy atmosphere for them to grow, by receiving early prenatal care, taking my vitamins, and actually eating more healthily than I did when I wasn't pregnant. As much as I wanted to keep them, it still did not change the fact that these babies were not meant to live any longer. Although my heart was broken, I still could not bring them back, which was one of my frustrations. I had a clear understanding of the eternal plan, but I still couldn't help wanting them back, thinking that would make everything all "right" again. I wished there was something I could have done to save them. I felt incredibly helpless.

Some of my friends were having babies the summer after Eric died. It was difficult seeing women have successful pregnancies, although I was genuinely thrilled for them. There were times when I would just break down and sob, feeling so sad and empty, and then I would tell myself to "buck up" and consider my other children and realize how thankful I was to have them. That thought did not take away the sorrow, but it did make it easier to bear.

For weeks, I was not hungry. I actually felt revolted when I even looked at food. Although I went through the motions of fixing meals for my family, I found that I had to force myself to eat, which given my usual love of food was quite unbelievable.

A few days after losing the baby, I felt desperate to rid myself of the incredibly empty feeling I was experiencing, and I wondered if taking a walk would help. Spring had definitely arrived, and although everything outside continued to appear drab and dreary to me, I still longed for some fresh air. Nearby there was a park, where a paved road, almost half a mile, encircled several soccer fields.

Change takes place one step at a time.

As I began walking, I noticed the contrast between my own silent discouragement and the excited bursts of joy coming from the young soccer players. I walked slowly about a fourth of the way around the track when I turned around and went home. Suddenly, I did not want to take a walk any more. I wasn't sure why. I just knew that at that moment, I didn't want anything except my baby.

The next morning was the beginning of another beautiful spring day. The fresh air brought a welcome relief to my dampened spirits. The warm sunshine beckoned me outside once more. However, I had the same experience that I'd had the previous day—I walked just a short distance before I gave up, turned around, and went home. With tears flooding my eyes, I wondered if I would ever feel better. I was quite familiar with the stages of grief and realized I needed to work through them. I just didn't want to have to experience the familiar, painful process.

The following week, after yet another restless night, I awoke to see the sun rising to greet a beautiful, fresh morning. I decided to try another walk. This time, though, I was determined to go just a little farther. I walked the short distance to the soccer park and began my trek on the path around the field. I got halfway around and found myself screaming inside, *No! I don't want to do this! I just want to be pregnant! I want my baby! I hate this stinkin' fresh air and I hate walking, and I'm going home!* With tears pouring down my face, I turned to leave. But after a few steps, I realized that it was the same distance to continue around the half-mile circle as it would be to go back. I stopped, and with great effort, turned myself back around. With each labored stride, I concentrated on taking just one step at a time. It was the first real exercise I had experienced in months. Because I had been so nauseated during the pregnancy, I had not felt like doing much of anything. Now, I had to admit, it was nice not to feel so sick, although I would have traded that good feeling in a heartbeat for the pregnancy, even if it came with the nausea.

Putting one foot in front of the other, I finally completed the circle. I felt surprisingly pleased with myself for having gone all the way around. I had walked half a mile! Although I was out of breath as I returned home, the fresh air and morning sunshine truly felt revitalizing. I decided I wanted to do it again.

The next morning, I was able to complete the circle again. Over the next week, I took some more early morning walks, going the same distance. During the next few weeks, I increased the time I spent walking, as well as adding a little distance each couple of days. It didn't take more than a few weeks for my daily walks to become a much-anticipated habit. For many previous years, I had enjoyed taking walks, but because my back and feet would throb so much, I wasn't very consistent, and I was also self-conscious of how big I felt, bouncing around the street. During all those years, I had wondered how I could ever lose weight if it hurt so much. My attitude toward exercise was not very positive. At times, I had also pushed too hard, wanting results right away, when it would have been much healthier to begin slowly and do it consistently.

Now I was seeing the positive effect of these almost-daily walks. I looked forward to that peaceful time, where I could sort out my feelings, work through my grief, even pray, as well as cry many tears. It was nice to know that it was okay to miss those babies and feel sad about what had happened. It helped the days go much more smoothly to take that time to think about my loss.

Those walks also helped me to understand that it was okay for me to feel better again. Life would go on and I could find joy once more. I had so much for which to be grateful. My belief in our family as an eternal unit strengthened me. What a comfort to know that we would someday all be together again. As I prayed more often, I pleaded for comfort and understanding. I realized just how essential faith and prayer are in our lives.

After a month, I still felt considerable sadness, but I sensed a small improvement. I *was* feeling a little better. One morning on my walk, I looked up at the sky. I noticed that it did not seem quite as drab as it had the morning I came home from the hospital. It now appeared a more vibrant blue. Even the sun seemed brighter.

Since I was not eating very much, I was losing weight rather quickly. After just four weeks, I had lost almost twenty pounds. I realized it was not healthy to be losing so fast, but I just wasn't hungry, and I was now walking almost an hour, six days a week.

Incredible enlightenment came as I took time out each day to exercise. Part of that illumination was recognizing—*finally*—the need to take better care of myself. If a family member or other loved one had gone through what I had, wouldn't I try to care for them in a loving way? Why not offer that same consideration to myself as well? After all, didn't I deserve my own best care—the same care I would have given to others? I began to realize I needed caring that only I could give myself. No one else could give me the care I needed most.

For many years, it had seemed that my body was not a true reflection of my spirit. It was almost as if my body was separate from the person I really was. I hated and blamed it for not dropping the weight I wanted to lose. I loathed looking at myself in the mirror. I was not making the connection that my body was just responding to my actions. For years, I felt as if my heart and mind worked together, but my body seemed to be working against everything I really wanted or knew to be true. The scriptural adage " . . . the spirit indeed is willing, but the flesh is weak" (Matthew 26:41) became very real to me. I wanted so badly to lose weight; I knew what I had to do to make it happen. However, for all those years I had regarded my body as my enemy.

Something occurred, though, as a result of the delivery of baby Eric. A few weeks afterwards, I was thinking back to the delivery and about how difficult it had been for the placenta to come. A light turned on in my head when I realized that my body, which I had been despising all these years, didn't want to give up the baby, either. What an incredible thought. *My body had seemed to be desperately hanging on to this baby, too.* That understanding softened my heart, and I began to think of my body in a new light. I still didn't particularly love it, but I was able to feel more compassionate toward it. Then I began considering all the wonderful things this physical body had done over the years. As a missionary in Bolivia, I had recovered after being very sick with typhoid. I also recalled how good the exercise I had done sporadically over the years had felt. My body had carried all my children, fed them, and helped care for them. I began to see my body, which I had loathed and hated to look at, in a completely new way. I found a new appreciation for it, as big as it still was. I did not love it overnight, but I started feeling differently.

It was an amazing thing to me, but my whole attitude changed. I wanted to take better care of myself. I realized I needed to have patience to be able to make such drastic changes. I found my body was very forgiving of all the years of abuse I had put it through with my eating habits and lack of consistent exercise.

> *Love and compassion can be stronger incentives than willpower.*

Another awareness came as well. When those babies died, part of me died, too. When I began to exercise and take better care of myself, I started to feel more alive again. That feeling was to become one of pure joy—of incredible peace. It was such a satisfying feeling that I wanted to experience it more often. I hungered for it. I realized I needed and wanted that joyful sensation in my life.

Things were definitely changing. I knew I wanted to live differently now. The lifestyle that I wanted included losing one hundred pounds, and I realized it would not come off immediately. I also knew I would have to put in an unbelievable amount of hard work and effort to make it all happen. At that time, I recorded in my journal, "I really hope that I can make this immense lifestyle change. When I think about eating less and exercising more and doing it for the rest of my life, I marvel at what an incredible transformation I need to make."

I realized battling my weight would most likely be a lifelong struggle. Even with all the willpower I could muster, it was *love* and *compassion* that finally made the difference. Changing my attitude, appreciating my body more, and feeling the incredible exhilarating effects of exercise gave me the determination to take on a fight that I desperately wanted to win.

And now, here I was, at the starting line of my first marathon, wearing a T-shirt and spandex running shorts, in a size Large instead of Double or Triple Extra Large! I had to pinch myself to make sure I wasn't just dreaming.

Then the countdown began.

CHAPTER FOUR

Getting Ready to Run

Bang! The starting gun echoed through the canyon. The marathon had begun! My heart was ready to jump out of my chest as I joined with the hundreds of other runners surging toward the starting gate. Because we began toward the back of the pack, Mark and I did not even arrive at the starting gate until almost two minutes after the gun had sounded. As I ran over the timing pad, for about the tenth time that morning I looked down at my timing chip to make sure I had tied it securely to my shoelace. My fanny pack felt a little loose, so I quickly cinched it tighter as I ran. We continued to move in one big mass, almost shoulder to shoulder, trying to avoid stepping on one another's heels and into any potholes in the road. A waft of fresh deodorant and clean clothes permeated the air. Huge floodlights lit our way at the starting line but grew dim as we made our way down the first hill. As the darkness enveloped us, I felt as though I had been ejected from the warmth and serenity of a comfortable surrounding into the cold yet exciting unknown.

Happy chatter filled the air, and it appeared that most of the runners shared my anticipation and excitement. I wondered how many of them also shared my nervousness. I felt like a scared kindergartner on the first day of school, excited but apprehensive.

I did feel a sense of reassurance, though. I knew the course well. Although I had never run the whole way, I had done some training runs over a few miles of the route to get a better feel for what I would experience today. And, over the years, I had run that racecourse a thousand times in my mind.

We passed Mile Marker 1 as we started up a long hill. I could faintly distinguish the outlines of runners further ahead, and I marveled at their speed. I thought about what I had learned from reading books and talking with marathoners. One of the first things they advised me was to begin the race toward the back of the group. That way, they explained, it would be more positive psychologically to pass (rather than be passed by) other runners. Another tip I was practicing was to begin at a slower pace than I usually ran during training. Mark said I could set the pace and he would just stay with me. I looked over at him again. I felt tremendous comfort just knowing he was there. As we continued our ascent, several runners passed us, and I wondered if we were starting *too* slowly. After the second mile, I wondered aloud to Mark when it was that we would begin passing other runners, as it talked about in the books.

That hill seemed especially long. I kept telling myself that I was here because I *wanted* to be here and that no one was forcing me to do this. I tried to keep my eyes just in front of me instead of too far up the road to see the incredible length of my journey that day.

I recalled the many months of training and planning for this moment. I realized that a key to my success in training for this marathon was having an effective plan. There were numerous programs and training schedules available; I had chosen one that worked best for me, which I adapted from a book called *The Non-Runner's Marathon Trainer,* by Whitsett, Dolgener, and Kole.

I realized how long and often difficult my weight-loss journey had been *and* continued to be, although the rewards far surpassed the anguish I had experienced. Having an effective strategy when training for a marathon is a key element for success; it is just as important to have an effective plan when losing weight. For me, holding myself accountable for my choices was an important part of my game plan. My weekly weigh-ins helped fulfill this need, as well as providing a way in which I could measure my success.

Easter came soon after little Eric was born. That celebration had always seemed like such a time of rebirth to me. Just as Jesus Christ was resurrected, I know we will all be resurrected as well. There seem to be varying thoughts on the question of babies who die before they are born and the matter requires a lot of faith. I firmly believe we will see this baby again someday, just as we will be together with Emily once more. These thoughts were of great comfort at that time, even though we still ached with grief.

We had leftover Easter candy, which, for the first time in my life, simply sat on my closet shelf. I did not even want it, although I ate some anyway, only because I could not believe that I could actually have unwrapped candy sitting there for weeks. It just was not like me. I also could not bring myself to throw it away. That would be wasteful, wouldn't it? I told myself it would come in handy sometime "when I needed a little treat to share with the kids." But I didn't really believe that. Sure, I might share some with them, but mostly, I felt comforted just knowing the treats were there and accessible.

After Eric was born, I was not hungry at all. Unfortunately, that feeling only lasted a month. By then I had lost almost twenty pounds, and the weight loss, together with my now-daily walks, enabled me to feel better physically. However, as the numbness of losing my baby began wearing off, my food cravings came back with a vengeance. I once again reverted to the eating habits I had practiced for thirteen years and knew all too well. I was surprised that although I was exercising on a regular basis and feeling better, the familiar attitudes still came back. I was once again using food to console myself. The numbers on the bathroom scale were now on the upswing. Of the twenty pounds I had lost, almost five had already come back. I saw myself once again spiraling out of control, and it scared me. I knew I was eating more than I needed, thinking it was helping me feel better. Even with prayer, exercise, and the newfound appreciation of my body, my habit of using food to cope with sadness, stress, and everything else was so ingrained it seemed an overwhelming task to break free from the ritual.

Perhaps the strongest emotion, aside from the pain I felt from losing another baby, was a familiar one—of incredible helplessness. I had already experienced Emily's death and had cared for Sarah and Hillary through their continued medical conditions. Eric's death seemed to be the final straw. There were elements in my life over which I had no control. I desperately wanted to feel I was able to exercise direction over *something* in my life.

For years, I had felt as though I could just lose weight by myself. Sure, I had tried many different ways, from powdered drinks or over-the-counter appetite suppressant pills to books and tapes on weight loss, but I always felt as though I could implement whichever program I was working on with enough determination to make it work. Time after

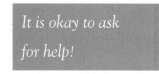

It is okay to ask for help!

time, I thought I could do it, and yet each time I had failed. It took me years to realize that what I was trying was just not working for me. I needed to attempt something very different. Quite a few of my friends had found success at Weight Watchers. I always resisted that approach by rationalizing that I did not want to pay anyone else just to step on their scale and be embarrassed. Besides, for years, I had told myself that I could not afford the investment.

Now, as I began to feel old habits returning, stronger than ever, I knew I needed to do *something*. I realized I couldn't afford *not* to invest in some help. I wondered if this could be the change I desperately needed. I felt better as I told myself that it was okay to ask for help. I also knew that if I waited much longer, I might talk myself out of it. It was a Wednesday morning when I called the Weight Watchers number I found in the phone book and was told there was a meeting nearby that night.

Making that phone call was one of my better decisions. A significant part of my weight-loss journey would consist of making myself accountable to another person. The leaders I met there were nice, and I didn't feel uncomfortable about stepping on the scale in their presence. I look back on that first meeting

I attended and can smile about it now. I made sure I left home early enough that evening so I could stop and eat before I had to weigh in. I went to Arby's for a large order of deep-fried mozzarella sticks as well as a large lemonade. I wasn't too hungry because I was nervous about this big step I was taking, but I ate it all anyway. It was one last hurrah. However, I did not stop there. Down the street, I dropped by Arctic Circle, where I downed a chocolate ice-cream cone. It tasted so good I went back for another. I wondered if the young women who were working there had a good laugh about the fat lady coming back for seconds. And that's all I could fit in my little tummy. I slowly drove to the building where the meeting was held.

I took my small tape recorder with me, which I had frequently been using to record my feelings. Once again, while I sat there in the parking lot, I voiced my thoughts: "I am excited and nervous, but I feel positive and want so badly to succeed. I hope I can keep this attitude. It is about 6:40 P.M. I am sitting here, in front of the Weight Watchers building, almost too afraid to go in. The meeting is supposed to start in five minutes. I don't see anyone else here but me. The glass is tinted, but I can see two women inside who look like they work there. Ooh, I ate too much. My body feels like it's ready to explode. Okay . . . here I go. This isn't very fun. Do I really want to do this? A big bag of chocolate kisses is sounding pretty good right about now. Over to my left, there is this skinny man just sitting there on a big planter, watching me, as it appears I am talking to myself. To my right, there is another man, also very slender, in a nice business suit, just walking around. I can barely stand the thought of heaving my body out of this car and waddling into Weight Watchers, past both of them. I'm so embarrassed . . . well, here goes nothin'."

At that point, I turned off my tape recorder and forced myself out of the car, tried not to think about what anybody who may have been watching me was thinking, and escaped into the building. I was grateful for the tinted windows. Before I could think too much about it, I prepaid for ten weeks. Although it was painful to lay that much money down, I *did* get a discount for paying for that many weeks, and more than anything, I knew I was committed for the next two and a half months. Resources were pre-cious enough that I knew I wanted to get my money's worth and give this program my full attention and commitment.

Taking responsibility for our actions is the first step in making positive changes in our lives.

I came out an hour later, after having taken a much-needed first step in finding a program that I hoped was a good fit for me. I actually looked forward to keeping a food journal and pausing before eating to determine the point value of the food. In the past I had inhaled food so quickly I had not even had a chance to fully realize what I was consuming. I knew it would take more time and effort, but I was ready for it. Although no food was off-limits, common sense told me that I simply could not continue eating the volume and kinds of food I had been eating if I truly wanted to lose weight.

I got back into the car, and although I still felt stuffed from my "snack," I was also feeling quite svelte in my size 4X black pants, since they were slightly looser than they had been a month earlier. Although I had already lost 15–20 pounds, according to the chart at Weight Watchers, I needed to lose 85 more. *That* was not a very cheery thought. In fact, it was, to say the least, *overwhelming*. I didn't want to think about it.

That first week I did pretty well. I wrote down everything I ate, and it was actually fun to determine the point value of various foods, based on calories, fiber, and fat content. I even made it through a delicious birthday luncheon that my mother put on for my aunt, sisters, and cousins. I actually felt healthier, even though my bathroom scale still told me I was morbidly obese.

The next week finally arrived. I went to the second meeting hoping to weigh at least two or three pounds lighter. After the meeting, I could hardly wait to get back to my tape recorder. **"YAAHOOO!!** I LOST 8.8 POUNDS this week!" I was shocked and couldn't believe I'd really lost that much. I was thrilled! The lady who weighed me said, "Now it's not going to be that same loss every week." I knew that, but I was still excited and felt even more dedicated. I also felt a little apprehensive. Could I really keep it up? Would my determination last? I knew if it were that important to me, I could really do it.

A few people told me, "You look good." They did not say anything about weight loss, and I realized that had a thinner person lost more than twenty pounds, it would really show. Since it was still difficult to keep a smile on my face, I also wondered how many of those people were saying nice things, trying to be encouraging after the loss of our baby. Whatever the reason, it felt good to hear their comments. I thought about the term that we often use when people have lost weight—saying they "look good." I think when those of us needing to lose weight finally lose a few pounds, it makes us feel so good that we radiate that feeling.

Almost two months after little Eric's birth, I had lost thirty pounds. Although I still had an incredibly long way to go, I felt great. When I looked in the mirror, I realized bulges that had once been huge were getting smaller. I still looked six months pregnant, however. How I wished I were! My arms still ached for my baby. Thankfully, the pain was diminishing a bit, and I was feeling better every day. It had not been easy. And I was in the process of changing my entire thinking about food. It helped to be able to focus on something positive, like my lifestyle change. Many times I felt a strong desire to sink back into my old habits. I was uprooting myself from my comfort zone. And were those roots ever deeply embedded! I knew that regressing to my old ways was not going to solve any problems. In fact, it would only create more. As I replaced my bad habits with good ones, the longing I felt for those old, familiar coping strategies would become weaker.

Reflecting on the progress we have made can be more encouraging than dwelling on the progress we still need to make.

After the first month and a half of attending Weight Watchers, I settled into losing only one or two pounds a week. I was working so hard, certainly as hard or even harder than I had been initially, when I was losing anywhere from two to four pounds per week. It was a little discouraging not to continue losing that much each time, but I had been warned that was what would happen. I found that my appreciation for my body was growing. I was taking better care of myself, and I was feeling much better in the process. Over the past decade, I had become used to all the junk I was putting into my body, and now I was making a major change. I realized that my body needed to acclimate itself to this transformation and that I just needed to be patient.

Exercising sure helped. Sometimes I would get the feeling that I was pounding myself around that track, trying to hammer out the hurt and the disappointment I felt about the loss of my baby. Working to feel better was hard. But it was worth it!

Some weeks later, I was washing my face. As I rubbed my cheeks, I could actually feel my cheekbones. It was the first time in *years* that I had been able to feel them! It was as if a dear old friend had come back into my life. There they were, my very own cheekbones, back from the obscurity of obesity where they had been hiding for so long. I was so excited I wanted to cry and squeal with delight. Was it really true? Or was I just reaching for some evidence of the success of my efforts? Although there was still *plenty* there, it was wonderful not to be able to feel so much flesh hanging on my body.

I soon discovered what feeling "satisfied" meant. For so many years, I had eaten until I was more than full. "Stuffed" was more like it. I was not proud of that. It wasn't a good sensation, but one to which I had become quite accustomed. My body was used to overeating. I now became increasingly aware that being "satisfied" felt much better. I began to eat more vegetables. Most of them did not have any point value, and it became a game to see just how much food I could get away with for the lowest points possible, without feeling as if I would pop. I was not eating sugar and large amounts of carbohydrates the way I had before. I honestly felt a little deprived because I craved those things! I looked forward to those cravings diminishing, as I had heard they would. I continued to realize that my whole thinking about food was changing.

As I kept losing weight, I had good days and not so good days. I was careful to write down what I ate, and there were times when I was pleasantly surprised that I had not done as poorly as I had thought. Although some days were better than others, the one constant that remained was my exercise.

72

Walking six mornings a week was an incredible blessing to me. I made it an essential part of my day because it felt so good and was so therapeutic. It helped me as I worked through my grief, thought about the past, and looked toward the future. I wanted to make sure I scheduled that walk into my daily routine. Some days it was very difficult. There were times when I was up most of the night with a sick child or up late talking with Mark or our older children. *Those* times were also important to me. I found, as I once heard Dr. Phil McGraw say about when he exercised, that on many of those mornings, "I was sure I was too tired to be out there." The incredible feeling of well-being I acquired from exercise, however, was much stronger than the fatigue. My appreciation for this physical body was continuing to grow. In turn, I was willing to be more patient.

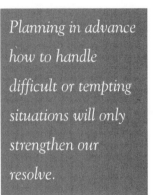

Planning in advance how to handle difficult or tempting situations will only strengthen our resolve.

During that time, I would not let myself give up. If I did not do so well on my eating one day, I would just keep telling myself that yesterday was in the past and I was going to concentrate on today. Instead of taking one day at a time, though, I found I had to take one morning or one afternoon at a time. There were some days when all I could focus on was getting through that hour, or that craving. I discovered I had to take one small step at a time.

By the end of that summer, I had lost forty pounds and continued to feel committed. Mark was telling me that he could tell I had lost a lot of weight. Finally, others were commenting as well. It sure took a long time, though, for anyone to actually notice I had lost weight! I just had to keep telling myself that I was doing this for me and not anyone else. But it amazed me how far I had to go before a difference could be detected.

I hit a slump after a family vacation that summer. When I picked up our vacation pictures, I was excited to see what I looked like in a photograph, after losing forty pounds. I was shocked when I could not tell any difference whatsoever. I thought there would be at least some change. My arms were still sticking almost straight out from my butterball body. I thought, "That's not me!" It was certainly not how I envisioned myself. Maybe it was the outfit I was wearing in the pictures. Yeah, blame it on the clothes. It seemed as though no matter how hard I tried, I just could not seem to look any better, even after losing forty pounds. Once again, I wondered if I was always going to look heavy.

The good news was that I was actually feeling great most of the time. There was also a huge difference in how my clothes fit. Seeing those pictures and not being able to discern any significant difference was quite discouraging. I tried to focus instead on how many positive changes I had made in my life. I knew that I would have to be willing to continue with these changes to not only feel the results but to observe them in the mirror as well.

One of the things I discovered was the importance of thinking through events and anticipating how I would behave in certain situations, especially with regard to what I ate. For example, one night Mark and I went to dinner at a Mexican restaurant with his brother, Scott, and Scott's wife, Peggy. I did not think ahead about what I was going to eat for dinner. Afterwards I wished I had chosen differently. I did eat fewer chips and salsa that came before the meal, which I considered a positive change. When it came time to order, however, I asked for something that I forgot was deep-fried. Usually, I would have eaten the greasy meal and felt overfull and even a little deep-fried myself. However, since I had made this change in my eating, I did not enjoy the dinner as much as I had hoped. Peggy, who takes great care of her health, ordered fajitas. That would have been a much better choice for me. It was a lesson to me, that I could learn much from observing healthy people, including what they eat.

> *We need to be patient and expect some discouragement and failures along the way.*

As time went on, I learned just which choices were the better ones. Fried and fatty foods did not taste as good as they had before. I still liked to eat them occasionally, however. I made many mistakes but found it reassuring to know that the important factor here was that I was learning from my choices, trying to do better the next time, and also trying hard to have patience with myself in making this significant change in lifestyle.

I continued to attend Weight Watchers. Although I was not necessarily learning anything I hadn't learned before, I was finally putting into practice the weight-loss ideas, and it was nice to see success. It was also reinforcing to hear from others who were struggling and to experience their success as well. When I fell, I got right back up. I discovered that each time I fell and got back up again, it made me stronger. One huge difference I was making with *this* weight-loss effort was that *I was picking myself up more often than I had before.* I still struggled, and it was not easy, even though I was losing weight each week. However, the good feelings that came from taking better care of myself made it worth the struggles.

On the eve of my birthday, I recorded the following:

"Tomorrow I will be forty years old. Last year, the year before, and many years before that, I would think on my birthday, 'This is going to be my year! I am really going to do it. A year from now I am going to be thinner.' However, I would realize, year after year, that it was just not happening. I often felt, as the years went by, that it was not *ever* going to happen; that I was sentenced to this fat body forever." Now things had changed. As I turned forty, I realized, "It is happening. IT *IS* HAPPEN-ING!" It was certainly one of the best birthday presents I had ever received.

As I continued to stick to my plan, it helped to focus on how well I was feeling as a result of the exercise and healthier eating, rather than paying much attention to the numbers on the scale. On those weeks when I had worked hard but had only lost a fraction of a pound, I realized that what really mattered in order for me not to get discouraged was how well I was doing in my daily endeavors, including exercising, writing down my food intake, and eating more healthy food.

However, one night late that summer, I calculated how much more I wanted to lose, and I became quite discouraged. I had already lost fifty pounds, but wanted to lose fifty-five more—more than the amount I had already worked so hard to shed. At that moment, it seemed insurmountable! I calculated that if I was to keep up this rate of losing one to two pounds per week, it would be late the following spring before I would finally reach my goal. And I wasn't even sure I could continue to lose that quickly.

(Nine months later, when, according to my calculations that evening, I should have reached my goal weight, I still had seven more pounds to go. It was now coming off a lot more slowly. Even though I wasn't quite at my goal, I was still encouraged that

I hadn't given up. And I was certainly closer to my target than I was that discouraging summer night!)

Later that fall, Mark and I went to San Francisco. I took a break from food journaling and watching every little thing I ate. After all, there were delicious pieces of cheesecake that I wanted to sample in a restaurant just across the street from our hotel, and I did not want to feel guilty! We also explored the piers, rode a tandem bike across the Golden Gate Bridge, and strolled together through the enchanting streets.

I loved San Francisco! We had a wonderful time. However, upon our return, I discovered I had gained two and a half pounds. I was disappointed, but still didn't feel bad about how much I'd enjoyed myself on that vacation. Instead, I knew I just had to dig in a little harder. I was able to get right back on track, and the following week, I was thrilled to see that I had not only lost those two and a half pounds, but another half pound as well. It was very rewarding to know that I could occasionally have a break without totally thwarting my efforts!

> *We will grow stronger each time we succeed at meeting little everyday challenges.*

I discovered that my commitment to my weight-loss program made it possible to get back on track if I slipped up and that it also carried over into other areas of my life. Facing everyday challenges seemed a little easier. I felt an inner strength, a peace, a confidence that I had not known before. The comfort I thought I felt from having leftover Easter treats on my closet shelf had been replaced with the far greater peace and reassurance I now experienced, knowing that I was the master of my situation. It was amazing. I was so grateful for the divine and earthly help I received as I carried through with my weight-loss plan, and I knew I could not do it without help. Little by little, with each step, I was realizing that I *was* doing it—I was accomplishing my dream! And, despite what I had thought for years, this *was something I could do!*

We could make out the "Mile Marker 2" sign, even through the darkness. Those first two miles had taken longer than I thought they would. Were we starting out *too* slow? Was I was just nervous? Mark was right there by my side, offering words of support and humor by telling me he would "try to keep up with me." It helped to think about anything else other than the reality of my present situation—the agony of running up a lengthy, rather steep hill at 5:00 in the morning, after not sleeping at all the night before, at the end of the pack, with twenty-four miles to go.

My commitment to lose weight was not unlike the commitment needed to train for the marathon. A high level of dedication was required for both. Desire was crucial, and some sort of plan was needed as well. *And the plan needed to be followed.* I felt encouraged because I had followed a marathon-training plan that prepared me for this adventure. I had started a weight-loss effort countless times over the years, but it was not until I raised the bar on my level of long-term commitment and came to regard my body in a more positive light, that I finally saw results.

CHAPTER FIVE

High-Priced Heaviness

We were approaching Mile Marker 4, but I was already thinking about the finish line. I had pictured it more than a thousand times. The occasions when I had actually been there over the years, watching Mark, were so exciting and full of emotion. I had often wondered what it must feel like to cross that finish line after running more than 26 miles. At last, I would discover for myself. I felt like a young child who had attended all my friends' birthday parties and had watched while they opened their presents, wondering if my own birthday was ever going to come. Now my birthday party was finally here, and I was going to experience the joy of opening my own gifts! After years of enjoying others' marathon successes, it was finally my turn. It was still difficult to believe it was actually happening. What would it really be like at the finish line? I assumed I would still be running, and not riding in the back of some ambulance. I thought about my family members who would be there to greet me. My children, my parents, and my sister Holly would be there. Mark's parents, as well as his sister Lisa and her family had left their homes in Idaho in the early morning hours to be there, too. My rising emotions brought tears to my eyes. There was my sister Jill who had come all the way from Boston to cheer me on. My sister Chris and her children had sent posters from Chicago—bright, encouraging signs that made us smile. An awareness of support from my family and loved ones intensified the love and appreciation I felt for them at that moment.

With sweat on my brow, I thought about my own effort to be here today. I had certainly paid a high price over the past year and a half. I looked around at my fellow runners. I knew they had also sacrificed greatly to get to this point. There is a high cost to run a marathon, just as there is to realize any ambitious dream. The expense is what makes the reward so worthwhile.

Yes, I had paid a high price to be there. I had also paid a high price during years of morbid obesity. I sadly knew what it cost in terms of lost self-respect, fatigue, discouragement, and poor health associated with being severely overweight. I had kept numerous journals during that time, and I was glad that I had recorded those thoughts, because I did not want to forget what it was like to be so overweight that it adversely affected almost every aspect of my life. I never want to go back to that lifestyle.

Although I had been telling myself for years that I did not want to stay mired in an obese lifestyle, I could not seem to break out of the vicious cycle. Instead of grappling with my challenges and frustrations directly and dealing with them in a constructive way, I tried to cope with them through eating. Because I consumed more calories than I was working off, I kept gaining weight. To counteract the depression over how I looked and felt, I sought comfort in more food. And the discouraging cycle continued.

It was as if I were on a merry-go-round that never stopped. Occasionally it was fun, and I certainly had a comfortable seat, or at least had created a definite comfort zone. But I desperately wanted to get off the ride. I watched as others stepped off, and many encouraged me to jump, too. I was offered countless ways and strategies to leave the whirling dizziness of the carousel, but I just could not seem to make any of them work for me. Occasionally I was able to step off for a moment, but then I would be whisked right back on, with the speed increasing each time. I could not understand. Why couldn't I just jump off and stay off? It was as though I had an infinite number of tickets and couldn't bear the thought of them going to waste. So I stayed on the huge machine, whirling endlessly around while hating what I was doing.

When I was at my heaviest, although I habitually avoided mirrors, one day I just stood and studied my reflection. I marveled at the size I'd become. I looked (and felt) almost nine months pregnant. Each morning it was a struggle just to heave my big body out of bed.

One of the greatest prices I paid for being so overweight was the body aches. For many years, I seemed to hurt *somewhere* all the time. My knees and back ached constantly. And my feet throbbed relentlessly. It was even difficult to simply bend over and tie my shoes, which I could only accomplish by holding my breath and exerting a great effort. To avoid the discomfort, I mostly wore slip-ons, which tended to be non-supportive and added to the throbbing of my arches.

Some mornings, my feet hurt so badly I could scarcely walk. Getting out of bed and walking those first few steps was excruciating. I winced in pain with each footstep. Getting some simple exercise such as just walking around the block was so incredibly painful that I didn't attempt it very often. For years, I did not go to a doctor because I was sure what he would tell me. I did not want to experience the embarrassment of having him say that my problem was simple to diagnose—my feet were being called upon to haul around too much weight.

However, the pain became increasingly worse. When it got so severe I could not stand it any longer, I finally went to see a podiatrist. I thought maybe if *I* mentioned the whole weight issue first, he wouldn't have to, and the visit wouldn't be so awkward. I explained I was trying to lose weight and I was walking for exercise, but that my arches were killing me. I was relieved to find him kind and sensitive and not at all judgmental. He gave me supports to put in my shoes, encouraged me to continue to exercise when I was not in too much pain, and to wear good, supportive shoes. I realized I needed to take better care of my feet. I needed to set proper time aside to care for myself. I just could not seem to do it.

On an episode of *Oprah* dealing with weight issues, there was a woman who weighed 320 pounds. One of the first things I noticed about her was her beautiful hair and pretty face. Nevertheless, it was heartrending and all too familiar, listening to her describe what it was like to be obese. She talked about using several pillows at night when she slept, propping up her stomach, legs, and back to get comfortable. I understood what she was saying, as I reflected on my own poor quality of sleep, and how I also found it more comfortable to use extra pillows. However, feeling comfortable as I drifted off to sleep did not happen very often. Most mornings, I awoke tired and feeling little, if any, effects of a restful sleep.

The woman on *Oprah* also said that she used a hose attached to a shower-head to properly cleanse herself after using the bathroom. As I realized her poor quality of life, I expressed tears of sadness for this woman. I had a few tears for myself as well. I wondered: *Is that where I'm heading, too?*

Keeping a journal of our feelings can be very helpful.

One day I recorded, "I'm tired of being fat. I guess when I get tired enough of it, I'll do something about it. Obviously, that has not happened yet. Today I did not have a shower. Why? The biggest reason is that it is so uncomfortable to get dressed. Every time I go over to my closet, I stand there, staring at my size 2X and 3X clothes, and I get nauseated. Nothing seems to look good on me."

I disliked most of my clothes. One item I did *not* loathe was a dress Mark bought me one Mother's Day, when I was at my heaviest. As I unwrapped his gift, I noticed that he had selected a beautiful spring pattern in yellow, my favorite color. I was thrilled he had chosen such a lovely gift. My next realization was the size—3X. I immediately felt sick. He said he was not quite sure of my size and had just guessed. My size up until then was only 2X (although it wasn't long before I was wearing a 3X quite comfortably!). However, that day, I actually felt a little insulted that he had not bought the smaller size, as if a 2X were all that more petite than 3X. I can smile about it now, but at the time, the dose of reality stung a lot. I tried to focus on his beautifully wrapped present, and the fact that he had gone out, on his own, and bought me a pretty dress. He wanted to surprise me and do something nice. I appreciated his gesture. More than anything, I felt humiliated at the thought of him going in and buying the biggest-sized dress in the whole store. Again, I was reminded, even through a thoughtful act, of how huge I was.

Shopping for clothes was painful, and I avoided doing it. If I did need something, I'd go to a department store nearby. Vowing that *this* time was positively the last time I would have to buy anything in the Plus-size section, I would ride the glass elevator up to the second floor. Gazing out at the racks and racks of beautiful, smaller clothes, I'd rest my forehead sadly on the glass and once again feel imprisoned in my big body. I did not have the freedom of choosing any of those lovely clothes. Sure, the bigger sizes were pretty, but I wanted to be able to fit into the smaller ones. Why couldn't I just *do* something about it? If my desire was so great, why couldn't I break free from my self-imposed prison? My guilt and disgust for myself increased.

One day I bought two new shirts. Usually it was a little exciting to get some new clothes, and it would be at least a few months until I started disliking them, because they constantly reminded me of my size. But that particular day, although I needed them, I despised those clothes the minute I bought them, because of how I felt while trying them on. When I got to the car, I disgustedly tossed them onto the seat, absolutely hating them already.

The far right side of my closet held my "dream clothes"— the clothes I had worn fifteen to twenty years previously. Some days I would get them out just to look at them. Occasionally I would hang them up in front of me while I was on the treadmill to give me inspiration. After being obese for so long, it was next to impossible—even comical—to picture myself ever really fitting into them again.

There *was* one particular dress. Oh, how I loved that white dress! I first wore it when my sister Chris got married. It was a beautiful summer wedding, and the dinner, held after the ceremony itself, was at Deer Valley, a ski resort nestled in the breathtakingly beautiful Utah mountains. What a lovely setting. And I felt beautiful wearing that dress. I adored my sister, and she was marrying a good man. The whole evening was magical and everyone seemed so happy.

I wore the dress only a few times after that day. As soon as I became pregnant with our twins, I outgrew it, but the dress remained a reminder of a wonderful occasion and a carefree time of life. During all those years while I was far too heavy to wear it, I occasionally took it out of the closet. As I lovingly touched the lace at the neck and along the hem, I often felt the tears as I remembered how I once was able to fit into that dress, and how I felt wearing it. How I wanted to be able to wear it again! A few times, I even put it on and tried to imagine being able to zip it up. The possibility of that dream coming true was unimaginable. Those were awful moments, and at times, I thought about giving the dress away because it *was* so painful to look at. It represented just how far off course I had drifted. However, I could never quite manage to give up the idea, however ludicrous it seemed, of one day being able to fit into it again. Even though it was difficult, almost impossible to imagine, I hung on to that vision.

A friend who also struggled with her weight once said to me that at the time, she weighed more than she had upon the delivery of her last child. I did not *ever* think I would get heavier than nine-month-pregnancy-status, without being pregnant.

Then came the day when I stepped on the scale and realized I, too, was there. I weighed more than I had when I was nine months pregnant with our youngest child. It was also thirty pounds more than I had weighed nine years earlier, just before I delivered my twins! I could not believe it. I was disgusted with myself.

During those years, I was also mistaken for being older than I actually was. One day, when I was about thirty-five years old, I was sitting next to my neighbor at church. He was a young man about nineteen years old. Another member of our congregation, whom neither my neighbor nor I knew very well, began talking to me about this young man in a way that made me realize he assumed I was the young man's mother! My neighbor and I were both embarrassed. It was discouraging to realize I clearly looked ten to fifteen years older than I really was.

Another day I went to get my hair cut. The stylist trimming my hair appeared to be in her early twenties, and she kept talking about what her mother liked in styles and hair products and wondered if "maybe you'd like them, too." I was only about fifteen years older than the hairdresser, but I must have looked archaic to her, as she kept referring to her mother. I consoled myself by thinking that her mother must be some cute young spring chick, but when I came back to reality, I knew the truth of the situation, that I appeared (and felt) much older than I really was.

One day at the store I saw a big shopping cart full of candy on sale. The price seemed too good to pass up. Looking around quickly to make sure no one could see me putting the treats in my cart, I quickly grabbed a bag of my favorites. At the checkout stand, I discovered that in my haste, I failed to notice that I had snatched the wrong bag—they weren't my favorites after all. To add to my predicament, they rang up for the full price. I told the checkout girl that I did not really want them. She assumed it was because they rang up at the wrong price, because she replied that she would ring them in at the sale price, which she promptly did, and plopped them in a bag. The checker should have honored my request and not given them to me. However, even more obviously, I realized I was not assertive enough. Therefore, I ended up with candy I did not want, and, shame to say, I ate it anyway.

On another occasion, I was walking on the campus of my alma mater, Brigham Young University. I saw a man with his four children and recognized him to be a student with whom I had worked fourteen years earlier. He saw me coming toward him, but he didn't look closely. Did he recognize me? And if he did, was he too disgusted to stop and talk? No, he seemed like too nice a person to behave that way. He must not have recognized me. I would have loved to have visited with him and meet his children. The only thing—the *only* thing—that was holding me back from calling out to my friend, was the realization that I was about one hundred pounds heavier than the last time he had seen me. It was a sick, sad feeling. My weight was holding me back from doing so many things.

One evening I was in a bookstore and saw Marie Osmond, who lived nearby. A few months earlier, she had divulged on her TV show that she was going through a rough time with postpartum depression. I thought she was very brave for speaking out about it and helping others in their struggle as well. As she walked by me that night, I wanted to say, "Marie, you go, girl. We're behind you all the way!" However, I said nothing. Because of my weight, I feared my gesture would be meaningless to her, that because I wasn't dealing well with my situation, I was disqualified from extending encouragement. I recorded, "I feel a stigma attached to my weight. I sense that somehow what I say is not as sincere as if I were saying it in a thinner body. But, when I think about it, when one of my overweight friends says something to me, I don't doubt *her* sincerity. So then why do I think I convey a different message with my own fatness that other heavy people do not? It is this perception that I feel about my body. This is not the 'real me,' but it is the one I am conveying. I have to get over this perception, whether I weigh 300 or 130. *Anyone* can be sincere, no matter what they weigh."

There were other missed opportunities as well. One day I recorded, "It is a beautiful morning! It just rained and everything outside smells so fresh. I was excited to go out for a walk. I put on my sweats and was just about to leave the house when I saw my reflection in the mirror. I looked so huge. My legs, especially my thighs, appeared so enormously fat, that I just could not bring myself to leave the house. I felt terrible to have missed such a lovely morning."

One evening I had to run some errands in the car. Mark said he was willing to stay home with the children, and I was frankly looking forward to a bit of solitude. But I was looking forward even more to stopping somewhere for a treat. One of my daughters wanted to go with me, but I told her no. I didn't want her to see me eating something I knew I shouldn't, so I left her home. It would have been a great opportunity to spend some one-on-one time with her, but I missed out on doing so because of shame. I sadly realized that day how very much my eating habits were adversely affecting me, even in my relationship with my sweet daughter.

Another night I had dinner with some high school friends whom I had not seen for many years. As I sat outside the restaurant in the car, I wished I hadn't eaten all those Tootsie Rolls I had consumed earlier that day. When I entered the restaurant and saw my friends, I noticed they all looked much the same as they had in high school. Sure, we had all aged a bit. But they all still looked great. I was the only one who really looked very different—almost one hundred pounds worth of difference. I felt so sad.

My twenty-year high school reunion was held soon after that. I had been looking forward to the event for years, thinking for *sure* I would be back to weighing at least somewhere near what I weighed in high school. I did manage to lose *some* weight. But when the weekend arrived, I still weighed eighty pounds more than I had when I graduated from Skyline High School. I knew I would love to see my friends again, but I cringed, thinking about facing them in this heavy body. I had a few friends, such as those in my dinner group, whom I had seen occasionally since high school. Because we had talked about going, I decided to go ahead and attend.

I'm so glad I decided to go. Others in my graduating class had experienced many tough situations over the years: divorce, unemployment, problems with children, and many of the men had lost their hair. There were even those who had also struggled with their weight. However, the overwhelming feeling I had was that we were just glad to be there and that we accepted one another just the way we were. I am so happy I attended!

To deal with the pain caused by emotional or physical problems, many of us seek to mask the pain by turning to drugs, alcohol, food, sex, and other substances. One friend shared with me that the awful feeling she gets when she overeats, as terrible as it is, is less severe than the emotional pain caused by her other problems. She realizes that eating is no solution and provides only a temporary fix, followed by remorse and self-loathing that she attempts to assuage by eating even more. That is exactly what I experienced for many years. It is such a vicious, nasty cycle, perhaps not fully understood by those who have never experienced a weight problem, but it is very real nonetheless. It is a monumental discovery when one realizes that more joy and fulfillment can actually come when we do not allow out-of-control passions to destroy our dreams.

There is tremendous confidence that comes from overcoming bad habits and conquering one's weaknesses.

For so many years, just like my friend, I gained much more satisfaction from food than I did from facing up to my trials. Although it is *much* easier said than done, how much more gratifying it is to feel self-mastery than to abuse food and other substances. There is tremendous confidence that accompanies overcoming bad habits and in conquering one's weaknesses. When I finally realized how much *more* positive the rewards were from healthy living than from continually practicing the bad habits I had cultivated over the years, I felt as if an incredible burden had been lifted off my shoulders.

There are people, women in particular, in abusive relationships. During the notorious trial of OJ Simpson, this issue was often discussed in the media. I remember wondering how on earth women could stay in these kinds of relationships, suffering physical and emotional abuse that is so severe that they need to be hospitalized. Many of these women would return to the same situation they were in before. That was difficult for me to understand. I was so grateful I wasn't experiencing abuse.

And yet, when I thought about how I faced one negative or humiliating experience after another because of my weight, I realized I was behaving in the same way—returning time after time to a situation I despised. Feeling powerless to change is a terribly helpless feeling. It was so frustrating to realize I had the power to change my situation but somehow couldn't muster the courage or the will to do it. Realizing my own weakness, it occurred to me, for the first time, how these abused women might feel. Although I will never fully understand what they endure, I think I know something of the forces that keep them from escaping the abusive situation they are in.

We should learn from the past, including mistakes, poor choices, and triumphs.

I missed a better quality of life during all those years of obesity. Sleeping uncomfortably, not being able to move without pain in the morning, and not being able to tie my shoes without incredible effort were just some of the simple things that affected my lifestyle. Shopping for clothes was also a negative experience. I cannot go back and reclaim those years. That has haunted me. I can only move forward. And *that thought* has motivated me and filled me with incredible hope and determination. I realize how important it is to learn from the past, including mistakes, poor choices, *and* triumphs. How essential it is to realize the power of optimism for the future! While hanging onto that hope, we can live each moment in the present better than we have in the past.

Although I truly admire those who are able to keep their weight under control, I also understand how quickly the number on the scale can head north. As I was losing weight, I felt shame for having allowed myself to get so heavy. However, I chose not to dwell on that fact. There were far too many positive experiences that I had as a result of my weight loss.

Remember the white dress I wore to my sister's wedding? I cannot begin to describe the elation I felt the day I put that dress on and it finally fit. I had to pinch myself to realize it was not just an illusion! This time I cried tears of joy. I put the dress on every day for a few weeks, just to zip it up and look in the mirror. It was hard to believe. It was actually *me* wearing it! My children were quite amused as they watched me try it on again and again. After experiencing many pregnancies and some southward sagging, I realize it will never fit as it did at my sister's wedding, but that's all right. My dream had come true!

Whew! There was another mile marker. We had completed the first five miles. Several of them had been uphill, just as many of my weight-battling days had seemed. I knew the road ahead would become easier, but there were still hills to climb. The first few miles of a long run were usually the most difficult.

Mark and I had managed to pass a handful of runners. I tried not to think about the two handfuls of runners who had passed us, even though we were still toward the back of the pack. Just as I did not want to forget any arduous moment of this marathon, I did not want to forget the pain of all the years of obesity, because the pain was great enough that I did not ever want to return to that lifestyle. I also knew that because of the endeavor, the wonderful, positive times would be that much sweeter.

The chill of the morning was beginning to fade as dawn approached. It was going to be a beautiful day!

CHAPTER SIX

Stereotypes and Humiliations

We were finally beginning our ascent up beautiful but narrow East Canyon. This part of the course was called an "out and back," where we were to run to a certain point, then turn around and come back down before climbing to the top of Little Mountain. I was looking forward to this part of the run because it was a few miles into the race, and on our way up the canyon, we would be able to see the front-runners as they flew by on their return. There was only a faint chill in the air now, especially with the heat we generated as we ran. Although the elevation was high, it was invigorating to breathe the crisp freshness of the morning. The sun was not fully up yet, but we could clearly see the runners now. I watched them with great interest. Focus and determination were evident in their faces, and the speed and pace they would hold for over 26 miles was amazing. To me, these athletes were "the running royalty."

They were young, not so young, short, tall, and they all appeared to have only a mere fraction of body fat. These elite runners stereotypically seemed to have the lean bodies of champions. I considered the stereotypes that often accompany those who are more than just a few pounds overweight.

There is no question that stereotypes attach themselves to those who are overweight, although many of these perceptions are incorrect. Overweight people are often labeled as lazy and incapable. It is not fair to assume that is true of everyone with a weight problem. Much of the population views fat people, particularly those who are considered obese, with disgust. This disdain may become worse in the future for those who are overweight as society becomes more aware of the health costs associated with obesity.

I have had many experiences where I was made acutely aware of the negative reaction to overweight people. Once I was speaking with a businesswoman who was telling me about one of her clients for whom she had done quite a bit of work. The client owed her a lot of money and was not doing anything to repay her debt. The businesswoman was an especially nice person, but she was also obviously frustrated; she felt as though her client was taking advantage of her good nature. In describing her frustration, the businesswoman mentioned that her client was "quite heavy," as if that fact validated her complaint. The client's weight clearly was not relevant, but her mentioning it was another reminder that a person's weight is often seen as an indication of a variety of shortcomings. And there I stood, in all my plumpness, listening to her story.

The grocery store was a place where I often saw disgusted looks aimed at me. One morning, I had a typical experience. I was at the store with Stephen, a preschooler at the time, and he wanted a doughnut. I knew a healthier snack would be better for him, but I was not a big doughnut fan, and I thought it would be a "safe" treat because I would not be tempted to take out any "Mama tax." While standing at the pastry bin letting Stephen make his choice, I glanced over at the nearby produce section. A woman, who I took to be about my age, was examining the apples. I immediately saw that she took immaculate care of herself. She looked as if she had been to the gym *and* the spa that morning. She had perfect makeup on flawless skin, and her jewelry matched her size-six outfit. After selecting some fruit, she scooted over to the vegetables. I felt very self-conscious, especially when she looked up from the broccoli and noticed me still standing in front of the pastries. She gave me a look of total disgust, as if to say, "What in the world do you think you are doing, looking like you do, buying doughnuts?!" Her look was real, and it made me feel even more self-conscious, to the point of feeling angry.

Stephen and I passed her several times as we walked up and down the store aisles. She sure had a lot of fruit and vegetables in that cart. Her nose was literally lifted high in the air as she passed me. I felt even worse. Angrier. Why couldn't she at least smile and say hello? But she wouldn't even look at me, let alone be friendly.

One of the aisles in which we passed was the candy and cracker aisle. There she was, selecting some little low-fat crackers. In my humiliation, I stopped and picked up a bag of cinnamon bears. She also went over to get some fat-free milk and yogurt, while I stood next to the "Buy One Get One Free" boxes of buttered microwave popcorn. "I'll show her," I thought, as I plopped a couple of those in my cart, too.

We finished our shopping, and I'm sure I bought more treats that day because of how I felt that woman looked at me. Clearly, it was a disgusted look. But then, I didn't know her. Perhaps she always had that same scowl on her face, whether she was disgusted or delighted. Maybe she didn't have any mean thoughts in her head, although that seemed pretty unlikely. I also realized that while she was unfairly judging me, perhaps I was unfairly judging her as well. At any rate, I was just glad she was not behind me in the checkout line to survey my cartload of calories!

That I was often viewed with disgust or disdain was not a figment of my imagination. For many years, I experienced the humiliation of unkind, hurtful glares as well as mean comments. I would react by getting angry at the insensitive person. But I was also angry at myself—angry and disappointed that I did not spend more time in the produce section, and less time buying sugary sweets.

I spent a lot of time rationalizing in those years. I always seemed to have plenty of excuses for not eating more healthy food, and I was always ready to lay the blame somewhere else. I thought that if I could just be more organized and go regularly to the grocery store, by myself, without children begging for junk food, I would make healthier choices. And, when I did not feel liked or accepted, it was easy to assume it was because I was heavy. I realized that even if I were of a healthy weight there would still be some who wouldn't like me, but it was easier to blame anything bad that happened on my weight. It did not seem to occur to me that I did not need to please everyone.

One key to my weight loss was that I finally felt responsibility for myself. I quit feeling as if my weight problems were the result of anything other than my own actions.

While there were many other times during those years when I felt others looked at me with disgust and judged me unfairly, I often wondered if *I* were the one judging the situation unjustly. Now, years later, I do not view heavy people the same way I was convinced that thinner people regarded me. Having been there helps me to realize what those who are heavy are experiencing. For example, during my years of obesity, when I would take walks, I was so self-conscious about what others must be thinking. Now, when I see a heavy person (or *anyone!*) exercising, I want to shout, "Way to go! You're doing great, keep it up!"

> *Wondering if people are judging us unfairly can be a waste of time and energy.*

Many times, I felt as if my body did not reflect my true spirit. One day I had an experience that made me realize that I was not portraying myself as the real woman I was. I had my three youngest children with me, doing some Christmas shopping. We had been on a few errands, I had bought them lunch, and we were sitting in the car finishing our meal before we went into a toy store. Just then, a woman and her children drove up and parked in the parking stall in front of us. The mother was quite large. She had on some sloppy looking pants, with a big belly hanging out over them. It did not look like she cared much about her appearance. She got out of the car and reached into the backseat to help a baby out of a carseat. Six-year-old Sarah saw her and, without batting an eye, said, "Mom! That lady looks just like you! She could be your twin!" My heart sank. I looked at this woman again. She was quite unkempt. My sweet little daughter, in her childlike innocence, was only telling me what she saw. I *did* look just like her!

After we finished eating and went into the store, we passed this mother a few times. Sarah whispered to me, "Look, Mom! There goes your twin!" Wow. It all hit me so hard. I was judging this woman by her appearance. And I looked no different! This woman was probably a very sweet and loving mother, as I wanted to think of myself. She probably had many wonderful talents and abilities, just as I thought I also did! I realized I couldn't see the good things about this woman. I felt humiliated and humbled to know that I came across the same way. Any wonderful qualities I had were hidden by this tremendous burden of weight, which was with me wherever I went, with me whatever I did, and my shadow in whatever I said.

One day I recorded in my journal, "I feel like I am basically a nice person. I try to have an optimistic outlook on life, and I think highly of people. But all these positive feelings seem to be hiding behind my body. My size speaks first. And it speaks so loudly! It frustrates me because no matter what I do or say to people, what I look like comes through much louder and clearer. It's not fair. It seems as though no matter how many nice things may come out of my mouth, it is because of the things that have gone *into* my mouth that my comments are dismissed. I know, I know, *life* isn't fair.

"But while we're on the subject of unfairness, there are many people who outwardly appear quite successful, but their lives are actually out of control. Some have addictions that wrack their very souls, but they can often hide their uncontrolled passions from the world. They feel torn apart inside and yet they can put on their 'game face' and appear as if everything is fine. Those who are not in control of their eating wear their weakness around all the time, like a huge cloak that is there *constantly.*"

I know now I was somewhat paranoid about the way I was treated, assuming that any slight or insult was a reaction to my weight. Most of the time, I only experienced the disgusted looks. But because of the many occasions when I was treated less than kindly, it was often hard to distinguish what was an unfair response and what was only a misguided perception on my part. For example, although I can smile about it now, one day the dental hygienist didn't give me a toothbrush as she usually did after a checkup. All I got was a lousy little piece of dental floss. I wondered. Was I just too chubby to deserve a new toothbrush?

Another humorous experience, although not funny at the time, happened one night at the drive-through of a fast-food restaurant. I wanted to surprise Mark by taking home to him his favorite caramel milkshake. I felt a little smug because I didn't order one for me as well. I was only getting a small chocolate ice-cream cone. However, I couldn't feel too proud of myself. I had just been to another fast-food restaurant, where I felt justified in picking up two French dip sandwiches because I had a "Buy One Get One Free" coupon. I had eaten one of them on the way to the ice cream store, and the other one was in my lap, waiting to be devoured. As I was waiting for the ice cream, I cleaned up the car a little bit. I gathered some garbage, including Peanut M&M wrappers (which were not mine), and put them on the seat next to me. Since I was driving a minivan, it was easy for the young woman who waited on me to see inside my car. She looked at the sandwich and the candy wrappers, then at me. As she handed me the ice-cream cone and the large caramel shake, there it was—that familiar look of disgust I had seen so many times before. But wait a minute! The shake and the M&M wrappers weren't even mine! I almost told her that. Would she have even believed me?

It made me think of a tactic that a friend of mine, who has also struggled with her weight, used occasionally at fast-food restaurants. When she would place her order at the drive-through, she would often ask for two drinks along with her large quantity of food, so the person helping her would assume my friend was ordering for two!

One evening I accompanied my daughter Amy in a concerto as she played in a piano festival. We had both worked many hours on the piece, and I was grateful that my mother had made me take all those piano lessons when I was younger. Although I wasn't totally confident with all the notes and realized that I might make a few mistakes, my biggest fear was getting up on stage feeling so heavy. Amy had wonderful stage presence. I don't think she made a single mistake. Her dynamics were incredible, and her interpretation of the music was superb. We both couldn't have been happier with her performance. Her hard work had truly paid off! Though I had been quite nervous, I think my part even sounded okay, too. I thoroughly enjoyed playing with Amy, as I did with all my children. Amy's piano teacher was there and gave her a smile, which I knew meant she also thought she had done very well.

Amy received a "Superior" score from the judges, which was a very high mark, and one of which to be proud. However, she didn't get any stars next to the "Superior," which would have meant the judges thought she went "above and beyond." And yet the performance couldn't have been any better. Although I felt good about the high score, I thought she deserved three stars. She didn't even get one. And here's the sad part; I felt somehow responsible. It was easy for me to believe that Amy had been shortchanged because of her overweight accompanist. They had misjudged her because of the way I looked. I was so disappointed for her. Amy seemed to get over it rather quickly. She was pleased with her performance and didn't seem bothered that she didn't get any of those sorry old stars.

I have to smile again when I realize how silly my thinking was! Those judges were professional women, a few of them with weight problems themselves. Of course they didn't withhold those stars because of me. And, as it turned out, when I talked with Amy's piano teacher later that night, she told me that Amy *had* earned three stars. The judges had simply forgotten to put them on the certificate. I had certainly jumped to conclusions.

Now that I am thinner, I am amazed at the time and energy I used to spend worrying about my weight and agonizing over how people would react to my size. For example, one day recently I was driving along State Street. I looked over at the car next to me and saw two teenagers, a young man and woman, smiling and laughing and looking over at me. I was not singing with the radio (as I often do) or even eating anything. I did not think I was having a bad hair day, either. Before my weight loss, I would have assumed without question that they were laughing at how fat I was. However, that day, I simply wondered what they had found so funny. Perhaps they were sharing a joke and just happened to look over at me at the same time. I felt confident that they were not laughing at my size, and, after years of humiliating moments of knowing (or assuming) people were laughing and talking about me, it is hard to describe how comforting it was to know they were not laughing at my obesity. It also made me wish people would be more careful about the comments and looks they give to those who are overweight.

There are many who do not understand what an overweight person is experiencing, including how very difficult it is to lose weight.

There were plenty of times as an obese woman that I experienced humiliation. A few months after Stephen was born, I had a particularly painful experience. My sister Holly was getting married. I was feeling huge, and with the weight I had gained during pregnancy, shopping for a dress was all the more painful. I felt and looked matronly in everything I tried on. I was hoping I could lose at least fifty pounds in the few weeks before the wedding so I would not look so poured into the dress. *That* didn't happen. On the big day, feeling so uncomfortably huge, greeting friends and extended family whom we had not seen for a while was difficult. I tried to focus instead on my darling sister and the nice guy she was marrying. This was *Holly's* day, and I was truly happy for her. I was also very aware of the delicious-looking smorgasbord of fruit, sandwiches, and pastries at the reception. I was very self-conscious about how I would look bellying up to the buffet table, and I didn't want to pop any buttons off my already-tight dress. Mark and I helped our three older children get plates of food, while I tried to keep baby Stephen happy during the festivity.

My sister Jill was recording a video of the evening, and I was trying to avoid the camera. Much as I loved my little sister and her cute new husband, I didn't want to appear on the tape. It almost worked, but toward the end of the reception, I was so hungry I finally got myself a plate of food. As I sat there, with a mouthful of éclair, Jill suddenly turned the camera on me. The timing couldn't have been worse. I had been so conscious the whole evening of trying to stay away from the buffet, and now here I was caught on film with a plateful of food in front of me.

Weeks later, the wedding party gathered to watch the video. Jill had done a fabulous job. It was delightful watching events of the happy evening, but once again the embarrassment mounted as I realized the only person on the video shown eating was—you guessed it— Plump Pammie. I knew Jill had not intended any ill will. She was only creating a joyful remembrance. But I still felt humiliated.

> We need to accept that there will be people who do not approve of us for one reason or another.

There were other embarrassing situations. One semester, after Hillary was born, I took a parenting class at BYU. The class was very informative, and it was fun to be back in the college setting. The only problem was the desks. I could not fit into most of them. Had I been able to hold my breath for the weekly two-hour class, I would have been okay. Since that was not an option, I had to arrive early enough to find one I could squeeze into without too much trouble. My main concern that semester was not the tough assignments and exams or even finding friends in class—my biggest fear was being able to fit at the desk.

One evening I experienced total mortification. Mark and I took our oldest son, just heading into his teenage years, to a meeting for young men and their parents, held at the church. There were no small children in attendance, and it was very quiet. At one point during the meeting, Mark had to go out for a few moments to make a phone call. When he returned and sat back down on the bench, there was a loud CRACK, as if the pew were about to break. I thought we were going to tumble to the floor. Although we didn't, it was *so* embarrassing. Everyone around us saw and heard what happened. Mark was a big man, but he certainly was not carrying around the extra weight I was. One young man, sitting nearby, laughed right out loud. The rest of the meeting I didn't dare move, for fear the bench would give way. I felt utterly humiliated.

Laughter and hurtful comments were commonplace. At a university football game one weekend, we started visiting with the spectators in front of us. We discovered the woman had graduated from my same high school, a few years after I had. I asked her if she had any older brothers or sisters I might know. When she told me her older brother's name, I didn't recognize it. She said that I probably wouldn't have known him because he was "a computer geek." Then this lady's husband turned around and, looking right at me, said, "Yeah, and you probably would have been able to beat him up!" Everyone around us (except Mark, bless his heart) laughed. I forced a smile but was mortified. Did his comment say more about the size of the "geek" or the size of my body? I couldn't tell. But I wondered if he made his assumption as he took one look at my fat face and fleshy frame. I could not imagine him making that comment to a thin person. Who knows? Maybe he would have. I thought to myself, "I shouldn't take his comment personally, because I'm really not that big." Then when I later noticed my reflection in the mirror, I realized, "Yeah, I *am* that big." I recognized that if it hadn't been for my weight, I would have laughed right along with everyone else, and would not have felt like the comment was directed at me.

One fall I noticed a good friend had lost quite a bit of weight. She had taken some over-the-counter pills to jump-start her metabolism. I thought, "Wow! Maybe I'll try them, too." So a few days later, I was at the mall doing some shopping. I went into a sports store because our son Nick wanted some short skis that year for Christmas. I always felt out of place going into a sports store, because I wondered if the employees would laugh at a hefty gal like me going into an establishment like that. I noticed the store security detector beeped when I walked in, but I didn't pay much attention to it. I went in just far enough to ask the first employee I saw if they carried short skis. When he told me they did not, I turned around to leave. The security alarm sounded again as I walked out the door, but again, I didn't pay any attention.

Just outside the store, I saw a booth where the same pills my friend had been taking were being sold. Thinking about her success, I walked over to check them out. I felt huge and embarrassed, seeking a magic pill to fix my weight problem. The price for one bottle of pills seemed outrageous, but I was so embarrassed to even be standing there, that I finally just said, "I'll take a bottle!" I glanced over and saw the manager of the sports store standing nearby, watching us, but I assumed he was waiting to chat with the sales clerk, who seemed to take forever to finish the transaction.

In my humiliation, I wanted to get out of there as fast as I could, and when the sale was finally completed, I started to quickly walk away. It was then that the store manager stopped me and said in a rather loud voice, "Uh, ma'am, would you mind coming back to my store and letting me know why the alarm went off on you?"

Embarrassed by the attention I had attracted, I walked back with him as the sales clerk and some shoppers stopped to watch this drama unfold. I timidly reminded him that I had only gone into his store a few feet to ask about the skis. I was so embarrassed, but I was very nice—perhaps even too nice—and I opened my purse and said, "You can look through here, I haven't taken anything." Thank goodness I didn't have any candy bars in my purse that day. I realized later that I should have been just a little more firm with him; after all, I had nothing to hide, except maybe the pills, but he had already seen me buy those. I looked back and noticed the onlookers watching wide-eyed to see if the big lady was going to get busted.

When the manager was finally convinced I had not stolen anything, I realized that I had beeped going in and out of a few other stores that day, as well. My sister Jill had given me a CD that I was carrying in my purse. Apparently, it was not "debeeped" when she purchased it. I teased her about it later, asking her if she really *had* bought it (she assured me she had). I was thankful I was stopped only once that day. But I will always wonder if he would have stopped me if I had been one hundred pounds lighter. How would *I* have responded if I had weighed less? Would I have been able to joke with him, even just a little, to make the situation less tense?

At most of the annual events I attended, I would tell myself that "by next year" I will be thinner. During the summer of 1998, Mark and I attended "Parent's Night" at Scout camp with twelve-year-old Nick. I thought that the next time I went up there, especially when climbing all the hills around the various campsites, I would for sure be healthier. Two years later, the next time our troop attended that camp, I was even heftier than I had been before. Mark and I traipsed around with our Scout, observing all the fun activities they had been doing during the week. After dinner, we hiked (and I huffed and puffed) up to the large amphitheater for the award ceremony. In attendance were about fifteen troops of boys, as well as many parents and leaders. A slide show on a massive screen highlighted the week's events, including the swimming competitions. The boys cheered wildly when it was time for the belly flop awards. The first honor went to a leader with a huge stomach. When his name was called, the boys and their leaders became even rowdier. Loud whistles and shouts erupted from the crowd. One of the adults yelled, "There was really no other competition!" Some of the boys continued to tease the leader as he went up to collect his award. "Wal-rus! Wal-rus!" they chanted, which seemed to be the name he had earned that week at the pool. He didn't seem to mind the teasing. At least he had a smile on his face. But I couldn't help wondering what he was feeling inside.

Just as the cheers were quieting down, I heard my name. When I turned my head, a boy who knew me was shouting, "*Mrs. Hansen* is the one who looks like a walrus!" I could not believe what I heard. But he had indeed said it. I immediately looked over at Nick and tried to laugh. He acted as if he didn't hear the comment, but I was sure he had. I am sure everyone around me had heard it. I was crushed. It was one of those moments where I wished I could have just disappeared under the dirt. For the rest of the evening I felt devastated. I wanted to go over and take a firm grip on that kid's bony shoulders and say, "How could you say something so heartless?" I wanted to scream and yell and take out my embarrassment and humiliation on him. I wondered what the rest of the Scouts would have done if I had stormed over and beat the soup out of him. That probably would have just given them all nightmares. The headlines would not have looked good either—"Fat Lady Beats Up Boy Scout."

Mark stayed at the camp to spend the night. I bawled all the way home. Here I was, a grown woman, feeling so humiliated about something a scrawny, little twelve-year-old had said. I felt silly for even feeling that way. But the real hurt came from thinking my own sweet son had heard the remark, too. I wondered if he felt ashamed of me. Or at least of my size. He was always so supportive and respectful of me and had never said anything hurtful, but I wondered that night how embarrassed he must have felt, too.

I wish I could say that the whole experience that evening had motivated me to exercise more and eat less. But as I recalled in my journal, I came home that night and drank a few quarts of chocolate milk. Nothing seemed to stop me. What was it going to take? I knew exactly what I needed to do. Why couldn't I just do it? Once again, I felt humiliated, helpless, and hopeless.

I will never forget an experience I had one time while I was traveling alone on an airplane. I boarded the plane, walked down the aisle, and, as usual, noticed some of the expressions on other passengers' faces, looking hopeful that the empty seat next to them did not have my name on it. That day I was glad I did not have to go far to find my seat, which happened to be on a row where there were three seats together. I sat down as quickly as I could, squeezing myself in the aisle seat, cinching the seat belt around my middle, trying hard to make it look effortless. (Who was I kidding?) The window seat was empty, and a small man with a pronounced New York accent sat next to me in the middle of the row. As I chatted with him, he smiled and was very polite. Although it was not a new feeling, I felt rather conspicuous because I was so much bigger than he was. I was hoping no one would come to sit on the other side of him, so that he could have a little more room.

Then a very large woman slowly came down the aisle. I was lost in my own embarrassment and didn't pay much attention to her. She stopped at our row, and, pointing to the empty window seat, said, "Oh, that's me over there." I immediately felt sick. I heard snickers from other passengers as they watched the little man and me stand up to allow this woman to get to her seat. It seemed as if there was a plane-ful of pity directed at this poor chap. I felt humiliated for myself and for him, and embarrassment in front of the rest of the passengers. What must this man be thinking, about to be sandwiched between two huge women? Was he wondering if he would even make it to Utah? Was it just my imagination or did he later pay extra attention to the flight crew as they instructed us how to get the oxygen masks down? My next thought went to the rest of the passengers. We were toward the front of the plane, so they could all see what was going on.

Drawing on our own life's experiences helps us have more compassion for others.

As we all sat down, my face was beet red out of embarrass-ment. I hoped we would not squash him. I quietly asked him if he would rather have the aisle seat. He just smiled and seemed to take it all in stride. I was so relieved he was not rude; that would have made it all much worse. He was a real gentleman. I will always be thankful for his kindness and sensitivity.

Out of the corner of my eye, I could see that our new seat-mate was struggling to get her seat belt on. It would not fit. She pushed the button for the flight attendant as I continued visit-ing with the man. I thought that if he was somehow able to continue thinking and talking about his family and life in the East, he would not be able to think too much about his predica-ment. A flight attendant at last answered this woman's call, and she quietly asked him for an extender. The steward yelled down the aisle to another flight attendant, "Hey, do you have a seat belt extender down there?"

I was so embarrassed. What if people thought it was I who needed it? This woman must have outweighed me by 75 pounds, easy. I was feeling ashamedly smug. I did feel "thin" sitting two seats away from her, noticing that her tummy reached out further than mine. The attendant came back with the extender for her. She sneezed, and the man said, "God bless you!" She thanked him, but other than that, she did not say a word. She took a book out and began to read. After a while, she put her head back and closed her eyes, but I don't think she was really asleep.

It wasn't until that point that I started thinking about *her.* Then I was absolutely ashamed of myself. What must *she* be feeling? I had been so caught up in my own snobbish shame that I hadn't even stopped to consider her. I felt terrible. If my seat belt hadn't fit, I wondered if I would have been too embarrassed and proud to ask for an extender. Would I have just laid the seat belt on my lap and tried to cover it up with a blanket or my purse? Perhaps this woman had a terrible fear of flying and that apprehension was worse than any disgrace she may have felt about her size, so much so that she was willing to ask for the extender, knowing how humiliating it would be to request one. I then wondered why she was traveling. Had she been to visit a sick relative? Maybe she had been helping a daughter who had just had a baby. There could have been any number of reasons. I was ashamed of my pride. Up until this moment, I had not even considered her feelings. Shouldn't I have been especially understanding of her situation? She must have felt mortified, especially when the steward yelled for the extender.

As a result of that plane trip, I promised myself that I would be more considerate. I hoped to have more compassion for people and be aware of their struggles.

I have gained a new appreciation for the difficulty of trying to cope with the incredibly vicious cycle of wanting so badly to do something about a problem that the resulting frustration only makes the problem worse. In my case, I would use food as a way of comforting myself against the frustrations associated with being fat. Those who have never experienced what I was struggling with might think, "Well, if it's so humiliating to be so fat, why don't you just lose weight?" As with many situations, unless one has actually been there, it cannot be fully understood.

I have friends who suffer incredible pain resulting from depression, chronic fatigue, and fibromyalgia. One friend has even wondered at times if she wasn't dying. I don't think I can fully comprehend what she and those who are similarly afflicted are going through, but I sure appreciate them sharing their experiences. How easy it is to judge others without knowing all the facts! I was also fascinated to learn from one of my friends how she felt that her physical body no longer reflected her true spirit. That is exactly how I had felt during all those years of morbid obesity. One friend related that because she could no longer do the things she had once been able and very willing to do, she felt those around her perceived her as "lazy," "unmotivated," and even "selfish." Having known her for many years, I am certain that she is *not* lazy or unmotivated!

I felt much the same way about how I thought I was perceived when I was so overweight. Although my sense of helplessness came from the health and lives of my children, I realized I had a lot more control over my size than my friends did with their health. One woman who had pushed herself so hard for so many years had come to resent that our value as a human being is often based more on *what we do* than on *who we are*. I've realized that much more could be written and understood on this topic!

Many stereotypes abound. Most of the time we do not know what others are experiencing deep inside themselves. We see them and their situations and often make unfair assumptions. Sometimes we can control or at least manage our challenges, other times, as much as we would like to, we cannot. I would hope that we would be more sensitive and understanding of one another, of those who are overweight or dealing with other challenges, whether they happen to be "controllable" or not, and whether those trials are visible or not so apparent.

As I thought about those incredible runners, now long gone, it sent a quiver of excitement through me as I realized I was actually sharing this race with them. I certainly did not have the stereotypical runner's physique, nor would I probably ever be bone thin. These top-form runners would finish in less than half the time it would take me, yet I smiled as I knew wholeheartedly that it did not matter. After all these years of watching from the sidelines, I was finally part of the race!

CHAPTER SEVEN

Taking Better Care of Mom

We passed Mile Marker 6. With each step of this "out and back" part of the course, I kept thinking the turnaround point must be just around the next bend. Then we would get to the bend, and there would be yet another curve in the road ahead. I had familiarized myself with almost every part of this course, traveling most of it in the car. I had even run a few miles, trying to get the feel of it. However, we were now in the only part of the course unfamiliar to me. By this time, there was a constant stream of runners passing those of us keeping a steady yet slower pace. I was amused to see men and women twenty, even thirty years older than I, who were running well ahead of me. The road just seemed to keep going and going. The canyon was becoming narrower with each labored, uphill step. Where was the turnaround? When could we finally begin our descent? When were we going to be done with this difficult part?

It took me many years to realize that I could take good care of my children and still take good care of myself. Taking better care of me did not mean I was neglecting their needs. In fact, I finally understood that having an emotionally and physically fit mother should rank high on the *child's* list of needs. It is not that the needs of the mother are at odds with the child's. In fact, the needs of the mother and the needs of the child are compatible, even linked.

I absolutely love being a mother. I had always wanted to be a mother, and from the moment I held my first child in my arms, I was thrilled with my new role. I have found motherhood incredibly rewarding.

As any mom or dad knows, there are also many times when being a parent is challenging and difficult. Early on, I found out what many women discover; that much of the challenge in being a mother is finding a balance between the time we spend taking care of our children and the time we need to care for ourselves. Because I mistakenly rationalized that my children always needed to come first, and justified that decision because of their health challenges, I neglected to effectively care for their mother.

Besides worrying about their health, I was caught up in the day-to-day routine of caring for my family. Cleaning, doing the laundry, helping with homework, going to ball games and music recitals, transporting the kids to the many places they needed to be, cooking meals, doing dishes, attending meetings at school and church, making phone calls, working on merit badges and science fair projects, and doing still more laundry—the tasks never seemed to end. Even with the help of a good husband and children, there was always something to do each day. And the next day it would begin all over again.

During the night, there would be a baby to feed, nightmares to calm, trips with a child to the bathroom, a drink to quench a late-night thirst, or administration of cough syrup or other medicine during childhood illnesses. Many mornings I would wake up and realize how desperately tired I still was. I fully understood and accepted that taking care of little children made for an exhausting time of life.

However, in giving my children my time and energy, I wasn't saving any for me. For years I wondered how I could make myself more of a priority in my life.

About three weeks after Hillary was born, I recorded, "Today I took a shower. It seems like it is the first thing I have done for myself in *days*. I stood there, feeling that wonderful water cascading down, and it felt so good I just cried."

I truly admire those who seem to be able to effectively juggle the demands of motherhood. However, I have also been able to sympathize with young mothers who felt, as I did for many years, overwhelmed at times by just everyday care that accompanies rearing a family. It is a fun and worthwhile job, but one that is also exhausting and demanding. I have friends who have struggled with other parental challenges. Some have given birth before they were physically or truly emotionally ready. Others have ached to have children of their own, and some have been blessed through adoption. Other friends have witnessed their children, after years of love and encouragement, make heart-breaking choices, but continue to offer love and encouragement. I have more fully realized that heartache for parents can take many forms.

Losing Emily and Eric helped me appreciate how precious children are. Watching my other children grow up so quickly made me aware that the time I had with them would be all too short. This growing awareness made the everyday challenges of caring for them more bearable and even more enjoyable.

Understandably, quite often, the needs of Sarah and Hillary have taken precedence over anything else. That would be true of caring for any child with a chronic physical or mental problem, and those demands can be incredibly taxing, emotionally and physically.

Like most people, I had a plan for my life. Among other things, my "Plan A" included raising healthy children. I hadn't given much thought to the necessity of the secondary arrangement of a "Plan B." I was quite caught up in living my dream of "Plan A."

Children's author Emily Perl Kingsley, who is the mother of a child with Downs Syndrome, captured the essence of what it is like to be living "Plan B." Her essay is entitled "Welcome to Holland."

> I am often asked to describe the experience of raising a child with a disability—to try to help people who have not shared that unique experience to understand it, to imagine how it would feel. It's like this. . . .
>
> When you're going to have a baby, it's like planning a fabulous vacation trip—to Italy. You buy a bunch of guide books and make your wonderful plans. The Coliseum. The Michelangelo David. The gondolas in Venice. You may learn some handy phrases in Italian. It's all very exciting.
>
> After months of eager anticipation, the day finally arrives. You pack your bags and off you go. Several hours later, the plane lands. The stewardess comes in and says, "Welcome to Holland."
>
> "*Holland?!?*" you say. "What do you mean Holland??

I signed up for Italy! I'm supposed to be in Italy. All my life I've dreamed of going to Italy."

But there's been a change in the flight plan. They've landed in Holland and there you must stay.

The important thing is that they haven't taken you to a horrible, disgusting, filthy place, full of pestilence, famine and disease. It's just a different place.

So you must go out and buy new guide books. And you must learn a whole new language. And you will meet a whole new group of people you would never have met.

It's just a *different* place. It's slower-paced than Italy, less flashy than Italy. But after you've been there for a while and you catch your breath, you look around. . . . and you begin to notice that Holland has windmills. . . . and Holland has tulips. Holland even has Rembrandts.

But everyone you know is busy coming and going from Italy . . . and they're all bragging about what a wonderful time they had there. And for the rest of your life, you will say "Yes, that's where I was supposed to go. That's what I had planned."

And the pain of that will never, ever, ever, *ever* go away . . . because the loss of that dream is a very very significant loss.

But . . . if you spend your life mourning the fact that you didn't get to Italy, you may never be free to enjoy the very special, the very lovely things . . . about Holland.

I had already discovered some wonderful things on my own trip to Holland. There was a sweetness that came from my sorrow, and a greater eternal perspective had arisen from my fractured dream of traveling to Italy.

I developed greater understanding and insight, and the satisfaction of caring for a family was very real. However, I still sought perceived comfort from food. The day-to-day demands were high. I missed my babies. It was difficult caring for Sarah and Hillary, and I was concerned for their health and worried about their unknown future. I felt as if I was always giving. I let my "bucket" drain far too often without pausing to fill it up. That is why, late at night when everyone else was in bed, I found so much enjoyment from eating. Most often, no one woke up needing me for anything, the phone and doorbell didn't ring, and the time was finally mine. By that time, I was exhausted and the food just tasted so good—or at least felt comforting. Then, a few hours later, when I would finally go to bed, I would feel sick to my stomach and mad at myself for eating too much and not getting adequate rest. Many nights it was hard to sleep, as I would try to figure out a way to get myself out of this late-night trap. And as I talked to other women, I discovered that I was not alone. I didn't seem to understand that life *would* go on even if I stopped to exercise, fix a healthy meal for myself, read a few chapters in a good book, or even take a relaxing bubble bath.

For many years, I rationalized that it would be much easier to lose weight when there were not small children demanding my time and attention. In reality, I only needed to look around and see just how many overweight people there are who do not have young children. In fact, I had an overweight friend who did not have children. As we discussed weight loss, I could not help but think how much easier it *should* be for her to lose weight because she wouldn't have children hanging onto her legs if she got on the treadmill. Then I realized she had other challenges to deal with that I *didn't* face; and I recognized that no matter *what* situation a person is in, it is difficult to lose weight.

Finding time for ourselves does not automatically mean that we are neglecting or taking time away from others.

Although I thought it would be much easier for me to exercise and rejuvenate myself when my children were all old enough to be in school, I did not want to spend my days wishing the time away. I wanted to enjoy my children *and* be able to conquer my weight while they were still young. I wanted to share my young children's lives as a "fit" mother.

My weight affected my role as a mother in many ways, both physically and emotionally. I know there were many times that I did not do things with my children because of how heavy I was. For example, I would have loved to go skiing with Nick, our oldest son, who was passionate about the sport. I had loved to ski when I was his age. However, in order for me to be able to go skiing with him while he was young enough for me to keep up with him, I would have had to get some adequately warm clothing. At that time, I'm not even sure they made them in my size. Worst of all, I knew I would have had to tell the guy at the ski rental place how much I weighed. That would have been absolutely humiliating. Even if I could just "grin and bear it," I was sure he and his buddies would be laughing as I walked out the door. Though I was thirty-seven years old at the time, I still didn't like the idea of being laughed at. Sadly, that fear of possible humiliation was stronger than my desire to ski with my son. And I desperately wanted to do that.

Emotionally, the humiliation and negative feelings of self-worth during my years of obesity magnified themselves as I tried to carry out my role as mother. For instance, we spent many evenings at the soccer field. Although I loved watching my children play sports, many of the other elements that came with it were painful. Those included trying to find something flattering to wear to the game, waddling out to the field, and cheering, trying to honestly show that sports and fitness, as well as supporting my children, were indeed important to me. Bringing soccer treats to the game was especially trying. When our turn came around, my kids enjoyed choosing the after-game treats, and although I sort of wished they would pick out something I didn't like, there were relatively few things that fell into that category. I also secretly hoped at least one kid wouldn't show up to the game, so I could eat his or her treat.

One day, in addressing a large congregation at church, a friend of ours mentioned that his wife was "just as beautiful as the day he had married her." I ached inside to think how much I had changed since marrying my handsome husband sixteen years earlier. I had gained one hundred pounds! Although I tried not to think about that little statistic too much, it hurt as I returned home. Once again, I would have liked to think it would have been motivation enough to get me going on some weight-loss effort, but it was just one more ugly experience to add to the heap.

Although I was not the least bit hungry, that day after church, I found the freshly baked rolls and moist chocolate cake quite comforting—at least while they were slithering down my throat. Like countless times before, I ate, trying to make myself feel better. Then I felt worse. There I was, spinning around on that familiar old merry-go-round. And, as I had so many times before, I wondered why I could not break out of the vicious cycle.

One afternoon I took my children and a neighbor girl to the grocery store. As I walked down one of the aisles, I noticed a woman coming toward us. She had medium blond, shoulder-length hair, the same color as mine. However, hers was dirty and unkempt. She wore glasses, just as I did. She had on a denim dress, like the one I was wearing that day. I looked down at mine; was it in desperate need of a good, sturdy washing machine as well? In addition, just as I was, she was obese. I denied to myself that I really looked that big, but I knew deep down that I probably did. A heavy man walked beside her, whom I assumed was her husband, because behind them walked a few chubby children. The woman clutched a box of animal cookies in her round fist. Halfway down the aisle, she plopped them on a shelf next to some potato chips. Then she nabbed a different package of cookies nearby and planted them in her cart. Further down the aisle, into the cart flew a few candy bars.

My daughter Amy and her friend Monica wanted to go to the makeup aisle to look at the lip-gloss. Smearing her lips with color was one of Amy's favorite pastimes. She even had a "lip smacker club," which included the neighborhood girls. Any time we were shopping, Amy felt as if the lipstick was calling—no, screaming—her name. We had almost finished our shopping, so I told them to go ahead, but to meet me in a few minutes at the cash register.

As I continued to gather the last few items on my shopping list, I happened to follow this heavy woman down another aisle, and, walking behind her, I could not help but notice her hips and bottom as they swayed back and forth, up and down. Is that really what mine looked like, too? I was horrified. My disgust was not for this woman, but for myself, because I knew that I *did not want to appear that way*. What happened next was just like getting ice-cold water flung in my face.

I was standing in the checkout line, and Amy and Monica came running up, exploding with giggles. Amy snickered, "Oh, Mom! Guess what just happened! I ran up to this lady, and I thought it was you, and I started telling her all about my lip smacker! She had this denim dress on, and glasses, and I thought for sure it was you!" . . . My heart absolutely *sank* as I realized my own daughter had mistaken this woman for me. Amy and Monica were not laughing at the weight of either of us—they were laughing about their childlike mistake. But I could not even smile. Their innocence spoke loud and clear. It was heartbreaking to realize that I really looked that large. Was I in denial? I honestly did not think I looked that big. I felt especially discouraged because I had even exercised for a few preceding days in a row.

One particular experience stands out as a perfect example of how my feelings about motherhood and my obesity affected me. Mark and I went to dinner with some of his colleagues. I wore what I called my "fat outfit," beginning with the size 22 white blouse, the size 24/26 skirt, all the way down to my size 4X "Control Top" nylons, which happened to have two large holes in them. Mark's department at work was considering hiring a woman who had a master's degree and was completing her Ph.D., and the dinner was part of a recruiting effort. I was really impressed upon meeting her. She was very personable, smartly dressed, and slender. I realized she was my age or even younger. I could see what an enterprising person she was, although she had made different choices than I had. She told me about her children and the nanny who took care of them as well as various other household duties. She seemed to be able to talk faster than I could even think. Although she was very nice and non-threatening, I felt intimidated by her position and knowledge. I thought about what I had done with my life. I had worked hard for the bachelor's degree that hung crookedly on the wall downstairs. I highly valued education, and recognized there were other ways of learning as well. But I also cherished the time I spent with my children.

Many thoughts continued to pass through my mind that evening. As I listened to this woman talk about the research she did, I felt out of place, quite uncomfortable—and as always—enormous. I thought about what I did during the course of a day. I guess I *was* involved to some degree in research projects as well. Part of my study included seeking improved methods of toilet training and exploring enhanced techniques of encouraging my offspring to execute their family stewardships (chores) and piano practicing without tears. I had discovered rapid and more effective ways of cleaning our habitat, as well as our apparel. However, when I compared my efforts, as important as I was trying to make them, with hers, they seemed never-ending and, for the most part, inferior. There we were, partaking of a delicious dinner, expressing well-deserved accolades, and celebrating her truly remarkable achievements.

My accomplishments as a mother, however triumphant, would certainly never be recognized in the same way. However, as intimidated, unimportant, and ignorant as I felt that night, I knew that the rewards of motherhood are richly fulfilling, often impossible to discern, and include priceless, eternal dividends.

I knew that *this* life was the one I had chosen for myself, and

I realized that I still would not trade my choice to stay home for the highest worldly honors available. I imagined this woman's life hadn't been easy, either. She had made difficult choices as well. However, I couldn't help reflecting that there were those who had chosen a different path, which seemed that evening to include a life much more glamorous than the one I was living.

Thoughts continued to run through my head. It wasn't that I blamed my heaviness on the fact that I chose to stay home with my children. Plenty of stay-at-home mothers do not have a weight problem. There are also many mothers who are employed outside the home who struggle with their weight.

It also broke my heart to see how my obesity sometimes affected my children. One evening I took my girls to a "Mothers and Daughters" retreat. The woman hosting it had a swimming pool. I watched as some of the thin mothers hopped in and splashed around with their daughters. I had parked myself on a poolside lounge chair, wearing as many clothes as I comfortably could to cover up my fat body, sweating to pieces, watching these women laugh and play with their girls. My daughters swam without me. They had encouraged me to get in with them, and I knew it did not matter to them that I waaaay out-weighed the other slim-bod mothers. But my pride got the best of me. I just could not bring myself to do it. As I sat there that evening, however, I wondered what was more painful—sitting out, not feeling like I was a very fun mother, or how I assumed I would feel putting on my Shamu-sized swimsuit, trying to appear invisible, while at the same time hoping there wasn't an incredible overflow as soon as my thighs hit the water. It bothered me that it bothered me so much. What did it matter if I was so much heavier than these thin mothers? Didn't I deserve to have fun with my daughters, too?

With these thoughts spinning around my head, I tucked my dear daughters into bed that night, and simply sobbed for the next two hours. I felt like a pathetic example of womanhood. My daughters had wanted me to get in the pool with them, but I was much too self-conscious. I felt bad for comparing myself to these other women and tried to think how many good qualities I possessed that had nothing to do with my weight. I just couldn't get myself to believe it wholeheartedly, because my weight, my lack of self-control, and the choices I was making regarding my health were all tied to so many aspects of my life. As hard as I was trying to take good care of them, I was setting a horrible example to my daughters in the way I was taking care of myself. I often felt like a slave to my appetites. That was not in harmony with my beliefs. I wanted so badly to master those cravings.

One day I went to a school banquet with then nine-year-old Amy. As I sat there in my too-tight dress, I looked around at all the other mothers, who all seemed so slim and beautiful. I was sure I was the heaviest woman in the room, which happened quite often. I looked at my darling daughter. I wanted so badly to be a beautiful, fit mother for her and for the rest of my children.

To add insult to injury, after the banquet was over the children put on a play. It was entitled *Advice to Parents!* and the kids acted out such ideas as "Parents, always give your kids whatever they want," as well as other "advice." Amy happened to be a narrator in a segment entitled "Now, Parents! This Little Piece of Advice Is for You. Always Exercise!" As I realized that was the only part on the entire program that was about exercise, it made me extremely self-conscious and embarrassed. Instead of sitting there and just enjoying my daughter, who was so cute and did a wonderful job, I kept wondering if people were thinking, "Gee, I hope Amy's mom is listening."

Another day I recorded, "Stephen's sixth birthday is today. I sure wish he could wake up to a physically fit mother. But he woke up, yet again, to a fat one, just as he has every birthday since he was born." My heart, along with the rest of my body, was heavy that day as I realized that my darling little boy had never known anything else but an extremely overweight mother.

Ironically, the pivotal point in finally commiting to the need to better care for myself came as a result of the birth—and death—of my last baby. When Eric came, I realized the need to set aside the necessary time to better care for myself. It was then that my entire outlook on life changed dramatically.

Soon after I began losing weight, I had a startling thought. I wondered how I would feel if I entrusted my child to someone I felt was a competent and nurturing caregiver. Suppose I returned home one day and discovered that my child had not been cared for very well, that proper attention and nurturing had not been given. It was easy to imagine that I would feel sadness and probably even anger. Here I had trusted this person to care for my precious child, and she had betrayed my trust. That's when I began to wonder, for the first time, how my Father in Heaven was feeling about how I was taking care of His daughter—me! I *hoped* He was pleased with the way I was caring for the children He had entrusted to Mark and me. But I had been so wrapped up in taking care of my family's needs, that I was not taking very good care of myself. And *I* am His child, too! I marveled at the recognition of the sacred responsibility I had, knowing Heavenly Father had trusted me to take good care of myself. My attitude changed as I gained a desire to show Him that I appreciated having this body and to demonstrate that I was taking good care of it.

Perhaps the most significant, most difficult, yet most effective step in my weight loss included rearranging my priority list. Taking care of myself had been far down on that list and often was not even there at all. I recognized the need to show more love and regard for myself.

I placed a new importance and higher priority on the hour or so I spent exercising each day. Whereas before I did not think I had time to exercise, I soon discovered how much *more* I could accomplish during the days when I *did* exercise. That investment in myself actually provided me with more energy to do the things I needed to do.

I also set aside more time to plan meals and snacks, and to plan ahead for those moments that had typically been difficult for me. For example, I quit asking my children what treat they wanted to take to soccer games. I just went ahead and bought treats that I knew I would not be tempted to eat. Imagine my surprise when I discovered my children were simply thrilled to be sharing a treat with their team. It did not matter that *they* had not chosen the snack, or that it wasn't the most popular treat in the world.

In the process, I was still every bit as involved in my children's lives, including helping them with school projects and going to games and attending piano recitals. I was doing some work from my home, volunteering at the school, as well as teaching the young women's group at church. I was also taking a home study class through BYU, which required a lot of reading and writing. I enjoyed doing it all. However, even with the reprioritizing I had done, I was feeling overwhelmed. I was very tempted—and succumbed a few times—to my old habits of stress eating. So I rearranged my time even more. I reprioritized the time I was not directly caring for my family by reducing my outside workload, cutting back on volunteering, and calling and asking the professor of my class for a two-week extension on a paper that needed more work. To my delightful surprise, the rearranging worked, and it relieved much of the pressure I was feeling. And things still got done!

I also made another astonishing discovery, which my family noticed. I made prayer an immense and essential part in rearranging my priorities and feeling comfortable with the time I was giving to myself. I realized I needed to put more trust in my Father in Heaven. Often I prayed for help in getting the exercise I needed, resisting the temptation to eat, and meeting the tremendous challenge of all I had to do, while still feeling comfortable with my mothering responsibilities. I was actually surprised by the outcome! I was getting the needed exercise and rejuvenation, my children were completing their homework, chores and piano practicing were getting done, they were getting to and from soccer practices, and I was part of it all. Our lives were *not* falling apart! What an incredible realization for me. My children were discovering that Mom not only needed a little time for herself but that she deserved it, too. Mark said more than once that I seemed happier when I set aside a little self-renewal time.

Besides putting more faith in God, I also put more faith in myself. I needed to give myself more credit. Instead of feeling negatively about myself and my abilities, I soon discovered that I could actually take care of my family effectively *as well as* myself. I wish I had learned this concept years earlier. I feel strongly that I would have been much better off had I made a little more time for myself during those trying years, especially squeezing exercise in as part of my day. It has made all the difference in the world.

However, it was not easy. I felt the need to pray even harder as I continued to exercise. At times, I was bombarded with children's pleas and problems the second I returned from a walk. Other times, when I was downstairs on the treadmill, I would hear arguing or Hillary crying. Even though there were older children to take care of her, it helped them to know I was nearby, and yet it was difficult for me not to jump right in

> *How essential it is that we take time to rejuvenate ourselves spiritually, mentally, and physically!*

and try to help them solve the issues. Turning up the TV or my music sometimes helped. The phone would also ring, and at first, it was hard for me to ask the kids to take messages. There were times, of course, when there were necessary interruptions, but they were few and far between. Most of the time, my children just had to learn to wait until I was through with my exercise. It took almost a year for all of us to adapt to this new behavior. I admit it was quite difficult—*but oh, so worth it!*

One day I recorded, "Today something significant happened. I did not get my walk in this morning, and the first opportunity I had to do it was this afternoon, after the older children had come home from school. When seven-year-old Stephen burst through the door, he was excited about a math game he wanted me to play with him as part of his homework. Ordinarily I would have been thrilled that he was excited about math, and I would have eagerly helped him. However, I knew it would take more than a few minutes to play the game. I faced the dilemma of helping him or taking my walk first. Soon it would be dinnertime. After I carefully considered our situation,

I decided to go for the walk. That was a totally new behavior for me. I left a slightly disappointed Stephen with his little jaw still open with surprise sitting at the kitchen table as I proceeded to take my 45-minute walk. I still could not believe I had made that choice. It was not like me! I had to realize that I was not being selfish; I was just putting myself on the 'front burner' for a while that afternoon, which was a huge step for me. I realized there is always going to be somebody who needs me—that just seems to come with the job description of *Mom.*

"When I got back from my walk, Stephen and the homework were still there. He and his friend Matt sat down and played the math game while I looked on, fixing dinner and helping them, when they needed it. They had fun and math concepts were reinforced. I reassured Stephen that his homework *was* important to me."

He had known that for years. Now he was also learning that exercise was very important to me. I was elated and surprised that it actually worked out that day, and it continued to work thereafter.

My family also learned to appreciate the healthier meals we were eating. I spent more time making up menus that included more vegetables than before, and it helped tremendously to plan ahead. The few days before a big run, we usually had pasta of some kind for dinner, as I needed to "carbo-load" in preparation. My kids would say, "Oh, Mom's going on a long run tomorrow—we're having spaghetti again!" Although my husband, a true Idaho farm boy, still loved meat and potatoes, I discovered that we ate meat more sparingly, and we realized we could live with that. We all felt better when we ate healthier.

In addition to the time I spent exercising, planning menus, and attending weekly Weight Watcher meetings, I also found time to enjoy other simple joys. I have always loved to read. My friend Kathy invited me to join her book club. I still remember the first meeting I attended. Looking around at the other women there, I realized this was not a PTA or church meeting, a doctor's office, or any other gathering where we were discussing the needs and activities of our children and others. This was simply a group of friends, women I admired and enjoyed being with, discussing our own thoughts and ideas. It was incredible to realize that I was a part of that group, taking part in such an enjoyable and worthwhile activity. I also wondered why in the world I had not done something like this before. Part of the reason was that I had felt selfish spending so much time reading a book or doing something pleasurable, just for me. I had gotten so caught up in doing the necessary things in my life that somewhere along the line I had not set aside any time to have a little more fun and enjoy life. The monthly book club meeting gave me a sense of euphoria. Here I was, doing something just for me!

Mark was incredibly supportive, and I felt better able to care for my family with more of a happy and peaceful spirit. I knew that for some, it was easy to find more and more ways to get caught up in activities in the name of self-preservation, and I realized I had to be careful. But I also understood there were undesirable consequences of putting everyone else first to the point that resentment could creep in and dilute the feelings of love and adoration I had for my family.

It took years for me to fully comprehend the concept of rearranging my daily priorities, including moving myself higher up on the list—and because of this new appreciation, I have felt much more peace. I generally feel more on top of everything. I agree with whoever said that if everything else during the day goes wrong, it is still a good day if you have gotten a good run in that morning!

I have to be honest. As my children have grown older, it has been easier to leave the younger kids in the care of the older ones while I exercise. However, there were many times when planning my weight-loss routine around my preschoolers' needs was necessary. When I began my crusade, just after having Eric, Sarah was experiencing one of her worst arthritic flare-ups, we had only known about Hillary's disease for a short time, and she was barely out of diapers. I discovered that a weight-loss effort could be accomplished with young children. I only wish I had reaped the benefits sooner.

As a result of this long, painstaking process, I realized that something incredible happened to me. Out of the reduced fat cells, a healthier mother emerged; a mother who truly *loved life*—who loved and appreciated her husband and children even more and who was better able to care for them as she took better care of herself. A much greater regard for good health came forth, as did more respect for motherhood, and the need to love, nurture and take care of not only the children, but also this significant person called *Mother*.

"You're almost there!" the runners shouted to us. I thought I could detect a hint of pity in their voices, for they knew better than we did how much further we really had to go to turn around. We were at Mile Marker 6. Half-full cups in some of the runners' hands and those discarded on the side of the road were evidence that we were getting closer. A water table was near! The more cups I saw, the thirstier I became. It was as if I had been in the hot, dry desert for hours without water and had finally spotted a large,

refreshing drink, with cold droplets clinging to the outside of the cup, and I knew it had my name all over it. The water table just ahead was like the benefits that came from taking better care of myself. In rearranging my priorities, moving myself higher up on the list, I discovered that the advantages of having a healthier, happier mother was just like a revitalizing drink of water during a thrilling, yet grueling marathon.

CHAPTER EIGHT

Footsteps of Focus

There it was—the water station! I wasn't sure I would make it. What a welcome sight. We'd had a few water and sports drink breaks, but this one seemed especially welcome. We would be able to turn around, run downhill (which could actually be more painful, sometimes), and give encouraging smiles to those poor people behind us. We gulped down some water, walked for a few minutes, and then resumed running. It was still shady, although all evidence of the darkness was now gone. High in the mountains, there was still a cool, dewy feeling in the air—beautiful running weather! If only we could hang onto these perfect conditions for a few hours. We still had a long road ahead. But now, heading back down the canyon, I felt exhilarated.

The next stretch of the marathon, miles seven through twelve, was actually quite pleasant. The weather was the best we would have that day, and I was enjoying myself, while at the same time trying to preserve my energy.

Then we arrived at Mile Marker 13. I considered the fact that we were only halfway. We had been running for over two hours. Some runners would have finished the marathon by now. Besides the awards and satisfaction, I thought of everything else that waited for them at the finish line—excited fans, body massages, ice cream—it was time to quit thinking so much about them and sharpen my focus.

My in-laws have a horse named Henry. Henry is a classic among horses. He is over twenty-four years old, which is old for a horse. During his lifetime, he has been a working cow horse, a backcountry packhorse, and a fun kids' horse for our children. These days, he is mostly a kids' horse.

Henry always appears to be well fed whenever I visit the farm. The reason for Henry's slick coat and portly girth becomes obvious any time the kids go for a ride. Henry's main focus is food. If there is anything to eat anywhere near his path, Henry finds it. He stops and lowers his head to take a few bites, often to the frustration of his young riders. Henry is not afraid to chase-off horses nearly twice his size to get at any feed thrown into their pen. The other horses have learned to respect Henry's obsession with eating.

I can relate to Henry's focus on food. For years, I spent most of my waking hours thinking about food-what kind I was going to eat and how I was going to obtain it.

At the same time, I had been fixated on my weight. Though I had not actually done anything about getting rid of it, concern and frustration had consumed me. Mine had not been a positive focus. It was instead negative and nonproductive. I was more concerned about the burden of feeling trapped by this extra weight and the adverse ways it was affecting my life, rather than what I could do to change things.

It was not until I changed both my focus and my behavior that I was finally able to see an incredible metamorphosis take place. For many years, I had waited for things to change on the outside, when where I really needed to begin making changes was on the inside. It was not until I changed my thinking about food and about my body that the immense transformation was able to take place.

> *Negative focus can be all-consuming and actually make the situation more difficult.*

During my years of obesity, I was overwhelmed by constant thoughts about my weight. My heaviness seemed to eat away at me. My back throbbed from carrying around all the extra pounds, and much of the time I felt exhausted and unable to move very comfortably. Losing one hundred pounds seemed an insurmountable task.

One day I recorded, "I spend close to every waking moment agonizing about my weight. Not just thinking about it, but actually agonizing over it. Why can't I do anything about it? I feel paralyzed! When I feel bad about something, I eat. When I feel happy about something, I eat. Food is an escape when things are not going well and a great way to celebrate when they are. Food seems to be a great way to flee the moment; and yet, it just exacerbates the situation.

"I think I should either be stressing over my eating and have it do some good, or I should just enjoy myself as I eat. However, I *can't* enjoy myself, because many times I feel out of control. That is not a comforting feeling."

The mental and emotional energy I spent agonizing over my

weight did me little good. In fact, it did a lot of harm. My self-esteem was low, I felt terrible about myself and my appearance, and since I was having so little success in this important area of my life, I had little confidence I would be able to succeed at anything else.

Yet, I felt strongly that I had been given divine potential, and there were some areas of my life about which I felt very satisfied. However, much as I hated to admit it, negative thoughts about my weight spilled over into everything else I was trying to do. Was there some way I could go from feeling overwhelmed by my obesity to having a healthy focus about weight loss and possessing a positive perception about my body? Somehow, I needed to change my negative, nonproductive focus into something positive and productive.

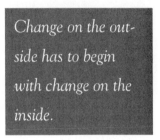

Change on the outside has to begin with change on the inside.

I made many lifestyle changes. Two significant changes had to do with focus. The first adjustment I made was to quit obsessing about the total amount of weight I needed to lose. Shedding that many pounds seemed impossible and was much too overwhelming. So, this time, although my ultimate one hundred-pound, weight-loss goal was always in my mind, I pushed it *way* back, and I made a conscious decision *not* to think about losing that much. Instead, I opted for smaller, more attainable goals, such as how much I could lose in a month. When that, too, seemed overwhelming, I tried thinking about a weekly goal. Many days I even narrowed my effort down to an hour or two at a time, which was much more manageable to me. If I felt like eating something I knew I would regret later, I made myself wait at least fifteen minutes before eating it. After that, if I still wanted it, I could go ahead and eat it, and I would still record what I ate in my food journal. Although it was difficult, after those (sometimes very long) fifteen minutes, most of the time I would realize that I really didn't want the tempting food enough to actually eat it. It also gave me some time to reflect on the effort I had put into my exercise that day. I didn't want to waste the hard work, and that helped in making my decision, too.

> *Focusing on the nature of the goal can be more effective than focusing on the amount of the goal.*

Something incredible happened as I disciplined myself in this way. During the waiting time, I felt empowered, knowing *I was becoming stronger than the temptation.* The increased strength also helped me be more steadfast the next time the temptation came around.

I began feeling successful in my efforts. As I continued losing weight, I was amazed at how wonderful it felt to be able to succeed at something that for so long I did not think I could do. I enjoyed the strength that I now realized I had been missing for so many years.

As I changed my focus to taking one day or even a few minutes at a time, I more readily saw progress, and I was able to enjoy success more often. Losing one hundred pounds has taken more positive focus than I ever thought I had. I continue to need that focus, taking one step at a time, as I battle to keep the weight off. Some days are much easier than others. Yet every day I find the need to rededicate myself. The self-discipline I developed from losing weight evolved from being a necessary part of my life to one that I have come to know as very desirable. Strength accompanies the ability to master oneself.

The second major change I made in my thinking was to

stop hating my body. For years, I had loathed my body as I struggled with my weight. I thought I would be fat forever—that my body was just incapable of losing weight. The spirit may have been willing, but the flesh was definitely weak. Inside I felt determined, but it seemed to me that my physical body was an enemy that would not make the changes my mind and heart wanted. It was as if there were separate entities at work within myself. Why couldn't we just all work together? The hatred I felt for my body kept me from thinking positively about any weight-loss possibilities.

Then came little Eric. As I mentioned before, when I lost him, I began thinking differently about my body. When I saw how difficult it was for the placenta to be delivered, I realized that it was not just my heart that wanted desperately to hang on to that baby. My body also seemed unwilling to let him go. I realized how much the human body can endure. Although I did not love it right away, I began having compassion for that long-hated physical part of myself. As I began taking better care of myself, losing weight and feeling better, I also realized how merciful the human body is. My body showed signs of being able to forgive me for the years I had abused it through excessive eating and lack of exercise. It absolutely amazed me how positively my physical self responded as I began eating healthier foods, decreased my portions, and got adequate exercise and sleep.

I am convinced that one of the keys to success at anything we do is the ability to stay effectively focused. During my weight loss, as positive focus became a more important part of my life, I thought of others who seemed to possess this quality. My friend Carolyn came to mind. I admired her so much. She related well with people, and she did an excellent job at whatever she attempted, both in and out of her home. She developed her own talents. Music and education were important to her and to her family. I wondered from the time I met her how she was able to accomplish so much and be as happy as she appeared to be.

Before I had gotten well acquainted with her, I saw her one day at the grocery store. We were both on the cheese and dairy aisle; I was at one end and Carolyn was at the other, and we were pushing our carts toward each other. I watched her as she walked down the aisle, hoping to catch her eye and say hello. I was interested to see that she was studying the food items very carefully as she walked along. She got all the way down to where I was without even looking around. I finally said, "Hi," and she turned and smiled, and we chatted for a few moments. As I thought about how intently she concentrated on her shopping, I realized it went beyond the aisles of the grocery store. Positive focus was a fundamental principle in her life. It seemed silly to recognize that from watching her as she shopped. However, as I came to know her better, I understood that to be one of her tremendous strengths. Carolyn had high expectations and set out to achieve them, with sights set firmly on her goals. Surely she experienced setbacks in her life; and yet she got right back on track and didn't lose focus of what she was doing.

Focusing is a way of not allowing distractions, which tend to make things muddled and blurry, to interfere. However, interferences are a major part of life. I discovered early on that distractions come with many jobs, particularly that of mother. In fact, it is as if one of the major job descriptions of a parent is dealing with interferences and distractions. Things do not always go as planned, and it is up to parents to be able to handle effectively the changes and challenges that arise.

One day, while I was taking a walk with my sister, we were talking about marathon training. A woman runner came toward us. She had a look on her face that indicated she was probably at the end of a long, difficult run. As she passed us, my sister whispered, half-joking, "Pam, when you run, will you do us nonrunners a favor and at least act like you're enjoying yourself?!" Although her comment was amusing, the more I eventually ran, the more I realized how focused a long-distance runner needs to be. The woman who passed us was incredibly focused that day. She appeared unaware of the

> *Smaller, incremental steps will lead you steadily toward your ultimate goal.*

people around her, and did not seem to mind that she was showing a look of great anguish on her face. I have seen that look many times on other runners' faces, and I have occasionally felt that same expression myself during difficult runs. There have been times when my body has absolutely ached, I have been tempted to quit, and I have had to search for strength to continue. But in the end, I'm always glad I kept going. For me, the satisfaction I get from running is worth the pain and discomfort. Now when I see runners who don't look as if they are enjoying themselves very much, I realize those looks also reflect concentration, determination, triumph, and perhaps even hope of a big cold sports drink waiting for them at the finish line.

In training for my first marathon, I participated in a few 10K and half-marathon races. I discovered there were key elements to having a good experience on race day. Preparation on my part was crucial. However, I realized other significant elements as well. For example, it was important to know that the race organizers had done their part. Before the event, the course had to be set up properly. Major debris needed to be cleared from the path. Signs had to be posted. I eagerly looked for those markers along the way, pointing which way to go, as well as informing me just how far I had gone. I looked forward to the water and power drink tables that had been set up along the route, with cups readily available as I ran past. I noticed that provisions had been made for first-aid assistance. There was sufficient, qualified help readily available if necessary. And certainly, a cheering section was always appreciated!

Any time I have thought about running a race, I have considered all these elements before I began. They are vital for any runner.

Strength results from success in mastering oneself.

I have discovered that the work of losing weight requires the same kind of planning as setting up for a race. Markers point the way toward more sensible eating habits and help me be more accountable. While running, I've often picked out an intermediate point—a rock or a bend in the road or a sign—and focused on reaching it, instead of visualizing the entire distance I needed to go. These short-term targets have helped me to enjoy success more often along the way. So, too, establishing a short-term weight-loss goal and reaching it provides frequent encouragement to go on.

I also made sure I drank adequate water during a race. Although slowing down at the drink tables and pausing at the porta-potties took time, they were necessary stops. Taking time to rejuvenate myself spiritually, mentally, and physically—including exercising, planning and preparing healthy meals, and getting enough sleep—was essential in my weight-loss effort.

First-aid is a critical need in any race. Taking proper care of the injured runner is vital. Many times as I was working to lose weight, I diverted from the path and fell. I found I needed to stop, assess the damage a bit, bind up my discouragement, and rededicate myself to avoid other possible pitfalls. When I would stumble yet again, I found it crucial to pick myself back up, give myself a few encouraging words, and keep going. And, just as runners appreciate those people designated to give first-aid and cheers, it has also been incredibly helpful to have others encourage me along the way.

Prepare for success!

The focus I had to develop as I trained for my first marathon helped tremendously in sustaining my determination to lose weight. Or was it the other way around? As I lost weight, did the focus I acquired help in my race training? It all seemed to intertwine. What an incredible feeling! I have discovered that a positive, productive focus certainly plays a significant part not only in running and losing weight, but also in anything we set out to achieve.

It was six miles to the mouth of the canyon, where Mark and I knew that our children and other family members were waiting to cheer us on as we headed into the last leg of the race. That thought motivated me not only to keep going but to run a little faster. I also thought about my Mormon pioneer ancestors, who traveled down this very canyon into the Salt Lake Valley so long ago. In many ways, they epitomized the courage, positive focus, and determination of a long-distance runner. Thinking of them gave me strength.

CHAPTER NINE

Magical, Motivating Moments

There they were at Mile Marker 19—our own little cheering section—jumping up and down and waving as we came out of Emigration Canyon. They were waiting there because it was a good place for us to stop and catch our breath, and there was a spot just off the road where the onlookers could safely stand and cheer. Amy, Sarah, Stephen, and Hillary were there, along with my parents and sister Jill, from Boston. My younger sister, Holly, was there, too, with her two daughters. Our son Nick was running the 10K leg of the race and would be waiting for us at the finish line. My dad kept taking so many pictures of us that I wondered if he thought we would even *make* it to the finish line. Mom kept offering us water, Ibuprofen, hugs, and encouragement. Our kids looked at us as if they were both amazed and embarrassed that their parents would attempt such a thing. Runners who had been behind us (I was a little surprised there *were* any!) continued to pass us, and we knew we needed to get going. The hugs and encouragement were incredible motivation that I would take with me for the rest of the race.

I still considered it a miracle that I had lost the weight, trained for this marathon, and was actually running it that day. I thought about the ways I had stayed motivated while losing weight.

Motivation plays a major role in accomplishing just about anything, especially weight loss. For years, although I felt motivated for the first few days or even weeks of yet another weight reduction attempt, I gave up rather easily after falling off the wagon; and then I felt discouraged and defeated. This was a reason I was not able to succeed at losing much weight. During the year and a half when I lost 105 pounds, although there were days I felt unmotivated and plenty of times I fell off the wagon, *this time was different*—I armed myself with artillery as I charged into battle, which helped me to get up, dust myself off, and bounce right back up onto the weight-loss trail. Although it was not easy, I had the overwhelming desire to make Sir Winston Churchill's motto my own, when he stated, "Never, never, never give up." I was determined not to give up.

These techniques, which were my arsenal, are the ones I used most, including some I have already addressed:

- Seeking and expressing gratitude for divine and earthly help
- Rejuvenating myself physically and mentally
- Having a plan and holding myself accountable
- Rearranging my priorities
- Replacing bad habits with good ones

- Recording measurements and feelings
- Staying motivated by trying on clothes in a smaller size
- Listening to inspiring music
- Making a dream/nightmare photo book
- Learning from life's lessons

#1—Seeking and Expressing Gratitude for Divine and Earthly Help

For years I felt as if I could lose weight "on my own." I had certainly prayed for help; however, I knew that no heavenly hand was going to appear and take food out of my mouth. Often I prayed to lose weight. I finally learned that the help is definitely there; but *I* had to be willing to work harder. I prayed for guidance to formulate a plan that would be right for me, and for the strength to follow it. I also got more specific in my prayers, and I took one day at a time. For example, I often prayed that I would be able to benefit from my exercise session that day, whether it was a 20-minute walk or a 20-mile training run. I prayed for strength to be able to make it through the morning without giving in to my cravings. What I discovered, too, was that I was praying more often than before. In sharing my successes as well as my stumbles in my prayers, I was also able to seek direction and discern the gentle guidance of a patient and loving Father in Heaven.

I also sought help from those around me, beginning with my husband and children. I had to change my lifestyle, which affected my family as well. It meant that the kids did not always get the carton of ice cream they wanted me to buy, because I knew there was a real possibility that I would devour it before dinner! It meant making more healthy meals, and even though my family missed the creamier, more fattening foods and snacks that we often had before, I sought after healthier ways of preparing food that would appeal to my family.

I also needed to be more vocal in expressing my needs. Getting homework done, practicing the piano, even attending children's soccer, football, and basketball games, now had to be worked around those things that I knew were essential for my weight loss.

In speaking up a little more for myself, the kids and I discovered that Mom was a person, too, and that I deserved some time to care for myself.

Expressing gratitude for the help I received was an essential part of keeping a positive attitude. I tried to focus more on the encouragement I received rather than on any negative comments I heard. As I began taking better care of myself, my gratitude for my physical body increased. Although patience was vital, I was amazed at how forgiving my body was.

#2—Rejuvenating Myself Physically and Mentally

Much has been said about the positive effects of exercise. Certainly, it is a necessary part of any long-term weight-loss plan. I discovered that when I took time to exercise, I felt not only physically but mentally invigorated as well. What an incredible feeling!

Hard work certainly paid off. Many times, I would set the alarm for 5:30 A.M., and as I dragged my body out of bed to go on a run, I had to remind myself how very important this run really was to me. The workouts, I discovered, provided a tremendous boost in my confidence and sense of well-being.

Mark's sense of humor was a welcome relief many of those mornings. During a run, he'd turn to me and say something like, "Honey, you're really pickin' 'em up and puttin' 'em down!"

Because it had been years since I had run consistently, I visited a neighbor at his running store. Hawk Harper, or "Mr. Running," as I called him, had run countless marathons. He gave me some tips, right there on the sidewalk outside his store. He showed me how to swing my arms to get more out of my stride and taught me to lean forward slightly to make my movements more productive. He watched me run, then offered helpful comments on how I could improve. I smiled, realizing how surreal this seemed; that I was actually running in front of this expert—or *anybody,* for that matter! A year and a half earlier, I could never have imagined doing that.

There is also a wonderful sense of inner peace that accompanies emotional rejuvenation. Time spent in quiet contemplation is essential to emotional well-being. It does not matter how many balls we are juggling or how fabulous we appear to the world; real success comes from feeling inner peace.

#3—Having a Plan and Holding Myself Accountable

Mark and I once attended a seminar on money management. The financial planner reported that the most significant element he had learned from counseling couples in managing their money was that no one plan was right for everyone. How true that is with weight loss as well. There is a plethora of weight-loss plans, with many touting that they are the best ones. I had tried most of them over the years and then felt like a failure when they did not work for me. Though I may not have followed them exactly as I should have, as I look back, I wish that I had figured out and developed my own plan based on my own needs and personality and what would work for me, not just which weight-loss plan was screaming the loudest at the time. It would have made a big difference.

One friend, in her weight-loss effort, found it helpful to eat only prepackaged foods, not having to measure or make any calculations. She lost weight, as long as she stuck with only eating those premeasured foods. Other friends used short-term plans such as drinking powder drinks for a few days, then going back to normal eating.

One element I knew I needed was to make myself accountable to somebody else. Having someone write down my weight each week and paying her to do it was sometimes painful. But to me it was an essential part in answering for my actions. I did not want to see that money go to waste. It also helped to know that I was going to have to answer for how I had done that week. Although many times my efforts did not show up on the scale, I continued to feel confident, realizing I was still moving in a general downward direction.

The plan I developed was one I felt good about, and I simply followed it. And I lost weight. When I did not follow my plan, I did not lose, or sometimes even gained weight. There were times when I had to be a little more patient when the loss was not as much or didn't come as fast as I would have liked. On those days when I did not feel motivated, I reminded myself that I really did not *need* to be motivated. I just needed to follow my plan. This simple internal dialogue worked! No one was more surprised than I.

One evening when I was especially hungry, I stopped at my favorite Mexican restaurant to get a grilled chicken salad. Served with rice, lots of lettuce, and delicious pico de gallo, it had become one of my favorites. I even preferred it without the sour cream. That evening, as I stood there in line with my mouth watering, I began thinking about what I had eaten that day. I was dismayed to realize that I was at my limit. Would eating the salad really make that much of a difference? Couldn't I do it just this once? There were days when I asked myself these same questions repeatedly. Although sometimes I gave in, this time I turned around and walked out of the restaurant, leaving my beloved unordered salad behind. I was hoping that I left a small piece of my behind, behind as well, by making that decision. Whew! That took some courage. However, I thought about the results of sticking with my plan, and that day, although I certainly wanted that salad, I wanted to stick with my program even more. I was glad I made that choice. While I knew that occasionally it wouldn't hurt, I also knew that saying no would only help me to be stronger next time. And indeed it did.

My plan also included writing down everything I ate. I told myself that I would write down *everything,* even if I ate more than I should. It was another way of holding myself accountable for my actions. If I was not truthful in my food journal, I would have been dishonest with no one but myself. And that integrity was of prime importance as I faced my weight problem.

A third element of my plan included drinking more water. Some days were easier than others to gulp down water, and while I was training for the marathon, I drank voraciously. I also discovered that my skin had a healthier glow as I drank more water.

#4—Rearranging My Priorities

Moving myself up higher on my priority list was perhaps the most significant and most difficult change for me. At times, I wondered if during many years I had even put myself on the list at all.

I found I had to say "no" a little more often. For so many

years, I had found it very difficult, and when I did turn down an opportunity to be of help somewhere, I felt enormously guilty. Others had quickly learned to call me because I was usually "available." Because of doing this to an extreme, it was also easy to feel resentful at times. Then I felt guiltier because I knew I would not enjoy the real blessings that come from service.

Because of always putting others first, I found it easy to shove my own needs to the bottom of my priority list. With young children, particularly with the health concerns of our two daughters, it was often necessary to consider them ahead of most other things.

In my quest to make time to take better care of myself, I have had to more consciously set aside the time to do it. I have also rearranged other areas of my life, even letting some things go, in order to accomplish this task.

For instance, I realized how I had changed direction in my actions and thinking. One morning I went on a walk, which was now part of my routine. A good friend and neighbor was also out walking, and as we walked together, she told me she was pregnant. She was nauseated and not feeling very well. I immediately thought of how I could help her, perhaps by taking care of her children more often or sending down a meal or two. There was nothing wrong in my thinking and desire to help her, but I knew I now had to have a few limitations on my time and efforts as I was also trying to better care for my own needs. There was a twinge of guilt as I realized I once would have jumped at any chance to help, even at the cost of my own well-being.

As was happening quite often during my weight loss, I realized I was making progress in rearranging my priorities. I was also more effectively learning some truths along the way. When

I returned home that morning after the time I had spent with my friend, I realized more fully that I could not effectively give what I did not have. I had to remind myself that although my family and friends were very dear and important to me, this time spent on myself was absolutely necessary. Now, when I offer help, even when it is at an "inconvenient" time for me, I am able to do so with a more cheerful and unresentful heart because I feel more emotionally charged and ready to be of service. There will always be plenty of opportunities to serve others. My perspective has changed for the better.

I continue to feel strongly that it is important to be of service and for our children to learn from our example of assisting in our churches, in our schools, and throughout our communities. It is also vital that we not judge one another on the amount of service we perform, realizing there is a time and a place for everything. While children are younger, we may not be able to do as much outside the home.

#5—Replacing Bad Habits with Good Ones

We are rewarded in some way by our actions. For many years, the pleasantness of food was my reward, my consolation, my celebration. I had to learn how to change my reward system and realize that the long-term compensation of a healthy body was more important to me than the short-lived pleasure derived from emotional eating. However, in order to entirely break the bad habits I had practiced for so long, I knew I needed to replace them with better, healthier habits.

For years, I regarded food as a reward. Like many people, the reward I acquired from food was greater than compensation received any other way. The satisfaction I received while I was eating seemed to make any worry or problem I was having disappear for a while, even though the issue was still there, in full force. The painful part was realizing I was not doing anything to help the problem and was even creating a bigger problem for myself with my weight gain.

Soon after Mark and I were married, I taught first grade. My young students' lives seemed to revolve around which holiday was approaching. The excitement of beginning a new school year in the fall soon gave way to getting ready for Halloween. Once that was over, they looked forward to Thanksgiving, and then of course Christmas. After coming back from a winter vacation, they got excited about Valentine's Day, with St. Patrick's a month later. By the time Easter was over, they were looking forward to summer vacation.

I am no different. I still eagerly anticipate the holidays as well. I loved (and admit I still enjoy!) all the food that comes with each holiday. I especially liked the candy on the store shelves during those times. Halloween was always a favorite, of course, because not only could I get just about any candy I wanted, but because of the cooler weather, I could also throw on a sweatshirt in an attempt to hide the result of my indulgence. Christmas always brought pretty red and green wrapped chocolate, and brightly wrapped bags of candy seemed to appear on the shelves the day after Halloween. However, I then faced the difficult decision of whether to buy leftover, much cheaper Halloween candy, or move on to the excitement of Christmas treats. Soon after New Year's, just long enough for my resolutions to fall by the wayside, the Valentine candy would emerge. Even before February 14th, Easter treats appeared. Then, for a few months when there was no major holiday to celebrate, I was not quite sure what to do with myself. Somebody got wise and started wrapping Tootsie Rolls and other chocolates in patriotic wrappers, so each year it seemed that there were more and more choices, with less time to have to wait between holidays!

I also had become accustomed, as my young students had, to telling time by which meal was getting close. When it was a quarter to twelve noon, I didn't regard it as "11:45 A.M." I thought of it as "almost lunchtime." Anytime in the afternoon was "snack time," or "just about time for dinner." It may sound humorous, but I definitely had to change my thinking!

As I considered my regard for food, particularly sweets, I made a chilling discovery one day. I had been talking to a friend who had a daughter struggling with drug and alcohol addiction. She described how her daughter was coping with situations in her life by reaching for harmful substances. As she described her daughter's addictions, I could see that I was in a disturbingly similar situation. I was reaching for more food than I needed to help me cope with life's challenges. It was chilling to recognize that I was also addicted—to food.

In my effort to lose weight, it became apparent how many bad habits I needed to replace. I had worked up quite a list over the years! I knew it would take some time. As I have already said, one of my worst habits was reaching for food when I felt stressed or worried about something. I also grabbed the easiest food available—usually something that I could eat without too much preparation. A bag of chips, bread, even a candy bar or two seemed available all too often. One habit I needed to establish was to plan ahead, including my meals and snacks, and have an alternative for when stressful situations arose.

It was important to me not to focus on the numbers appearing on the scale. One little ritual that I practiced nearly every week went against every weight-loss program I knew, as well as my new reward system. However, it was one of the most powerful incentives I had during my weight loss. Each week when I attended Weight Watchers, I weighed in. If I had lost weight that week, I treated myself on the way home to a chocolate ice-cream cone from a nearby fast-food restaurant. It wasn't a very big ice-cream cone, but boy, did it ever taste good! I did not allow myself one the weeks that I did not lose weight. It was hard to drive right past the restaurant, and it was amusing to me how much I looked forward to those ice-cream cones. I thought about them quite often! I also did not get them any other time during the week, and I didn't even count them in my food journal. It was simply a treat that I thoroughly enjoyed and anticipated each week. It helped in times of temptation, too, because I would tell myself that if I ate something that I knew I shouldn't, I might not be able to get that ice-cream cone. Stopping there was so enjoyable that I know it helped me to do better.

I certainly rewarded myself in nonfood ways, too. For example, when I reached one of my weight-loss goals, I bought myself a food scale to more accurately measure my food intake. I had wanted one for a long time, and I looked forward to that day when I finally bought the scale. I used it often, too, until I was more able to distinguish portion sizes. Every so often, I still get it out to make sure I am accurate in my measurements.

After many months of losing weight, I recorded: "Every day is a struggle. I think to myself, *Should it still be this hard? After 85 pounds?* Then I realize it may be somewhat of a challenge my whole life. I have heard some people say that it is not all that hard to lose weight. For me it *is* challenging. I am hoping that as I continue to live this different, healthier lifestyle, it *will* get easier. Some have encouraged me to think of it as something I *want* to do, not something I *have* to do. Not only do I desperately *want* to do this, I feel like I *have* to do it, too, for my health, my sanity, and my well-being. For *me*. For my little angels in heaven. For my children and husband *here on earth*. This weight-loss effort has been something I have had to consider through most of my waking moments. Right now, I have to consistently think through, plan my meals, exercise, and organize my life to make this weight loss happen. This is the first time I have put so much energy into the weight-loss process. But it is also the first time I have been able to lose weight and keep it off."

I discovered as I continued to lose weight and keep it off, replacing bad habits with new ones became a little easier. I found that the more I integrated the new plans into my life, they did not require as much effort as they originally had.

I loved rewarding myself. One day I took the afternoon off. I arranged for a friend to watch Hillary until the older children would get home from school, and I went to a movie, first stopping for a veggie pizza on the way, which was delicious *and* healthy. What a fun day that was! It boosted my spirits and recharged my batteries.

Another change I made was to pack some healthy snacks when I knew I would be away from the house for more than a few hours. It took time to cut up vegetables, and the kids thought the pretzels I'd brought along were for them, too. Soon I was in the habit of looking ahead to what my circumstances would be in a few hours (i.e. I'd be hungry). Having some healthy choices along to tide me over until I got home made a huge difference. I was not as tempted to buy fast food or a candy bar, and it saved money, too.

Another bad habit I replaced with a better one was the amount of sleep I got each night. I quickly became aware of how important adequate sleep is when trying to lose weight. Some nights, particularly those when I was waiting up for teenagers, were more difficult than others to sleep as much as I needed. For example, the night before a long run I usually was too excited to sleep very well. I certainly slept better the next night, however. Some evenings, although very difficult at first, I had to choose between leaving the house messier than I ordinarily would and getting to bed at a reasonable hour. I also worked harder at delegating cleanup to the kids. One night I recorded, "There are often times when I need to remind myself of the importance of my weight loss and that it means even more than always having a clean house. Right now I am committed to a healthier me."

Another change I made had to do with my hair. For years, while Mark and I were students, I had been going to the cheapest place I could find to get a haircut. I usually had a coupon, too. I wouldn't bother getting a shampoo or blow-dry, choosing not to spend the extra money on myself. I reasoned that "as soon as I got thin" I would somehow deserve to spend more on myself. How wrong I was in my thinking.

Occasionally, my sweet mother treated me to a few hours with her stylist. The other times, however, as I left the hair salon with wet hair, I disliked the job they had done. Perhaps it was mostly that I was simply embarrassed about my appearance and didn't like looking at my oversized face staring back at me in the mirror. When I looked at myself as I got my hair cut, I often thought that it was not really me in the mirror. I looked like a big blob with two beady little eyes peeping out. I knew I was in there somewhere, but it was as if I were lost underneath all that rounded skin.

In my renewed commitment to take better care of myself, I

wanted to find a hair stylist who would do a nice job cutting *and* styling my hair. I had lost about forty pounds when I called a nearby salon. I told them I wanted a hair cut from their best stylist. They told me Jaime would do a great job. One of the first things I noticed about Jaime was that she was very positive and smiled a lot. I felt pampered and even pretty when she finished. Although her prices were reasonable, I was paying more than I had before, including a shampoo and blow-dry. I had to keep telling myself that I deserved this good treatment, and that I was worth every penny. I also noticed something wonderful that day. For the first time in years, the mirror did not show a bloated face. My double chins were definitely there, but I was not looking into the mirror at a puffy, fat face—simply a fat face. It made me excited to someday see a nonplump face looking back at me from the mirror. Sitting there getting my hair done with my clothes fitting a little more loosely was a fabulous sensation! Jaime has been cutting my hair ever since. That simple change increased my motivation to continue with my weight loss. I also knew that since I was cutting my children's hair, it was okay to spend a little more on myself. I also decided that fat or thin, I was worth a little extra time and effort. I wish I had believed this concept years ago.

One terrible habit that definitely needed replacing was overeating to the point of feeling stuffed most of the time. As uncomfortable as it was, and as ashamed as I am to admit it, it was a feeling to which I had become quite accustomed. During the time I was trying so earnestly to lose weight, there were occasional times when I overate enough to feel stuffed. On those rare occasions, I remembered the familiar sensation, but now recognized it to be a very unpleasant feeling. I was amazed that for so many years, I had gotten used to feeling overly full. When I adapted to eating only enough to feel satisfied, what a discovery it was to understand how much better this sensation felt.

A good friend shared her insight with regard to this awful feeling. She realizes that she, too, is an emotional overeater. However, she also contends that the bloated, stuffed feeling she often gets as a result of eating too much is better than having to face the truth of her challenges. I came to despise that stuffed feeling, and when I discovered that the unpleasant conse- quences of my overeating finally outweighed my reluctance to make the effort needed to effectively deal with my problems, I finally began to lose weight.

#6—Recording Measurements and Feelings

One of the most powerful incentives in my weight-loss effort was to take my body measurements. I had been recording them for quite a while before I began losing weight. It was such a delight to see the diminishing numbers. In all, I lost over sixty- six inches.

Recording my feelings while I was heavy as well as during the months of weight loss was tremendously therapeutic. I wrote some feelings down in a journal, and others I recorded in a small tape recorder that I kept in my purse. I took the tape recorder out quite often as a thought popped into my head. I then transferred those thoughts by typing them and adding them to my journal.

Some early journal entries included the following:

"We went to a BYU football game today. When they announced the players' names and weights, I was horrified to realize that I weighed more than most of those big, old burly football players!"

Another entry read: "I often notice my cute friend Lisa out walking her dog. Some days she wears snug-fitting workout clothes. I get a lump in my throat, wishing I could actually wear clothes like that to work out in and dare to wear them out in public, even if it is just to go for a walk around the neighborhood. How incredible that must be! I admire the way Lisa looks so fit. I would love to feel as fit as she looks."

As the pounds came off, I was also excited to record my thoughts:

"There were many highlights of my dream trip to London with Mom and my sisters Chris and Jill. I laugh as I realize that one of the major highlights for me began on the plane ride, as I was finally able to fit comfortably into the seat! For years, I could barely squeeze my hips between the two armrests. I have always loved traveling, but just thinking about the tight fit on the airplane always put a damper on the anticipation before the trip. However, this time I could actually fit. I even wiggled comfortably around and still had room to spare! It was such an incredible experience that I would have been happy to just sit there for the fourteen-hour plane trip and then turn around and go home. I wasn't sure I could have any thrill greater than sitting and fitting in that seat."

Yet the thrills continued on that trip. One highlight was running in the parks of London. I wrote in my journal, "I ran through Hyde Park, St. James Park, Regent's Park, Green Park—what an incredible adventure it was to run almost every morning! I even wore my spandex workout pants in the subway to get to the parks, and although I was somewhat self-conscious, as I had not worn my 'Lisa pants,' as I called them, out in public before, I tried not to worry too much about how I looked. After all, I was going to exercise. As I looked around, there certainly were many others dressed in similar attire. For me, it was definitely liberating to wear that kind of clothing to work out."

Another entry: "In London we attended various plays and musicals. I saw *Les Misérables* for the first time in my life and fell in love with the music. We also went to museums, and spent many hours walking through magnificent displays of artwork. I absolutely loved it all. However, even though these were amazing experiences, especially sharing them with my mother and sisters, I have to be honest in admitting that one of the greatest high-lights for me was *not* hauling around an extra one hundred pounds. Many days, even though my feet ached from walking so much, I felt as if I could go on tirelessly for many more hours."

I also wrote: "I more fully realize how beautiful the human body is. Not necessarily how the world depicts the body as beau-tiful, or that my own body is particularly such beauty to behold, but I am even more convinced than ever how amazing the human body is."

On May 21, 2002, I was at Target, when I had this experi-ence: "They were having a sale on my favorite yogurt. A cute little boy, about six years old, was ahead of me in line with his mother. He surveyed the fifteen cartons of yogurt in my shop-ping cart with wide eyes. He looked at me and asked, 'Are you really going to eat all those?' I could not help but smile at him. I nodded, 'Yes, I am!' He looked at the yogurt, then back up at me and said, 'You're gonna get fat if you eat 'em *all!*' Perhaps some would have taken this as an insult. However, I was thrilled! He said I was going to 'get fat' if I ate them all, which meant that he did not see me as fat *now*. That was a huge compliment. From an honest little six-year-old."

Here's another entry that reflects how the "new me" was reacting to the changes: "On Sunday, our neighbor David spoke in church after returning home last week from a two-year church mission to Germany. Later that night, Mark and I visited him at his house. He greeted us, and I gave him a neighborly hug. He stepped back and said, 'Boy, you've shrunk!' I was a little uncomfortable as he and his family continued talking about how 'skinny' I was. I realize I am not very comfortable in this 'new' body, and I have certainly never been considered 'skinny.' But I thought David's comment was cute."

Here's another: "Tonight, when I saw a friend I had not seen for about eighty pounds, she looked me up and down and asked with a big grin, 'Good grief! Where's the rest of you?'"

Soon after that evening I attended a family party where I saw cousins whom I had not seen for many months. They couldn't have been cuter as they cheered, spun me around, and applauded my weight loss. What great motivation!

Here's one last journal entry: "A few days ago I bought some candy at the grocery store. Before, I would have been so worried about what the store checker would be thinking and embarrassed that he or she was probably thinking this fat lady had no business buying candy. But that day, it was nice not to be heavy and buying candy, all at the same time. I also realized that it did not seem to matter to me *what* the checker thought. I am thrilled to recognize that what others think of me does not matter as much as it did before. I also notice that my size is not standing out so much anymore. What a great feeling!"

It is helpful to reflect on the negative feelings and experiences I have had through this whole process. It's a lot more fun thinking about the positive ones!

#7—Staying Motivated by Trying on Clothes in a Smaller Size

Trying on clothes was, for me, a tremendous motivation. It was fun to just go into a store and try clothes on, even without buying anything. One evening, I went to a local department store. I needed some new pants desperately, since the only pair of pants I could fit into had large holes between the legs where my chubby thighs had rubbed together and worn them right through. Lovely visual, isn't it? That day I tried on some new pants and was *so* thrilled to be able to fit into the size 24, one size lower than my usual size 26ers. Every few weeks I would go in to see how the 22s fit. One day they actually did! I was so excited that I wanted to keep going and I told myself that I would not buy the size 22s, but when my stomach was "small" enough to fit into the size 20s, I would buy those. I clearly remember the day the 20s finally fit. Not only did they fit, but they weren't even tight! I was so excited! I had to laugh at myself, feeling so delirious that I could fit into pants that were size 20. That size is not exactly petite—but it had been so long since I actually had size 20 of anything on my body, that I was ecstatic. I recorded, "I never imagined I would even get back to this size. For years, I have looked in the mirror, thinking I will be doomed to this fat body forever! Today it was as if I saw a little glimmer of light at the end of the tunnel! It was so exciting. I have lost fifty-two pounds. To think that I still have over fifty pounds to go to reach my goal is overwhelming—so I'm just going to focus on the success I've had and move forward, one step at a time. I was so thrilled to try on a shirt (even though it was size XL) from off the rack with the 'S-M-L-XL' items. It has been twelve years since I have done that! Hooray! What will really be exciting is to someday be able to go and buy a size Large."

The wonderful experiences kept happening. One night I went shopping for a dress. Since I had not shopped for myself in any other department but the Plus-Size, I asked a saleswoman where the dresses were. She pointed me to the "Misses" section, without even mentioning the Plus-Size section. She made my day! And what an inexpressible thrill it was to try on clothes from the smaller-sized section, and to have them fit!

If I ever got feeling a little too proud of my efforts, however, one of my children would come along and humble me a little. One day, after I had lost almost two pant sizes, I was excited and rewarded myself with a much-needed belt. While I was putting on the new belt, seven-year-old Stephen came in and watched me thread it through the loops of my pants. He remarked, "Whoa, Mom, that sure is a loooooong belt!" I laughed. Just when I thought I was doing so well.

#8—Listening to Inspiring Music

Uplifting music has been a tremendous part of my weight-loss process. I have always had a passion for music. It can be soothing, encouraging, and very influential. I have come to realize how important it is to seek positive, uplifting music that inspires and elevates and helps us feel better about ourselves and our situations. Music can be extremely powerful, and although many avid runners don't use music while they run, I absolutely love to "tune" while I trot!

#9—Making a Dream/Nightmare Photo Book

I put together a book of photographs that I divided in two sections. The first section contained pictures of me in my early twenties, at a healthy weight. In the second section there were photos of me during my heavy years. Those were painful pictures to look at, and I avoided them at the time. However, after I had lost over fifty pounds and I could see a difference in those "before" pictures, looking at them inspired me to continue. I took that book out quite often along my journey. It was extremely encouraging to view the pictures and recall how I felt at the time the various pictures were taken. The visuals helped me to know I never want to go back to that weight.

#10—Learning from Life's Lessons

Taking the opportunity to learn from life's lessons is essential to our growth. Although it is not necessary to read something into every facet of our lives, it is important to discover what we can about the etchings of our existence.

Many experiences in our lives happen for a definite purpose. Learning what that purpose is gives meaning to our suffering; and what a shame it is when we refuse to learn what God would have us discover. Often we must travel to the depths of despair before we are prepared for this tutoring.

I learned much through losing Emily. When Eric was born, I wondered what more I needed to learn from losing a child. Hadn't I already endured this lesson? I didn't think I had slept through class, either! I became even more determined to glean everything I could from his death. The eventual sweetness that came out of the sorrow of losing these beloved children was, for me, otherwise unattainable. A loving Heavenly Father knows what we need to learn. He is there to help us, pick us up when we fall, and is ready to guide us, as painful as it may be sometimes, through our tutelage.

Much of what I discovered after losing Eric evolved with my greater understanding of the significance of self-mastery. I had dwelt in a state of utter helplessness regarding the death of Emily, the health of my children, and finally little Eric's death. I realize there are many things over which we have no control. We cannot do anything to change some aspects of our lives.

And that's okay. There *are* things we *can* control. How much more productive our lives can become if we focus on those things we can change for the better. One of the major aspects of our focus can be how we react to the problems and challenges we face every day, and discern all that we can from life's lessons.

Some say the last half of running a marathon is the final six miles. Experiencing the excitement of seeing our family now gave way to facing this ultimate test of strength and endurance. I felt recharged as we said good-bye to our loved ones and continued running, now heading onto the University of Utah campus. I had driven this same road many times with Sarah and Hillary, to doctor's appointments at Primary Children's Hospital. For many years, I had worried as I came along here, thinking about the issues facing our children. Now, tears of joy overcame me, as I celebrated the fact that this time I *was not* bringing a child to be examined, and that they presently were doing so well. That thought motivated me even further.

CHAPTER TEN

Getting Back Up
after a Fall

Mark was not doing so well. We had just passed Mile Marker 22 when he became unusually thirsty, and nausea swept over him. He had to stop running and walk quite a bit. The temperature had risen rapidly, and the heat was getting to him. Earlier in the race, he had waited for me as I ran at a slower pace. Now even that slower speed was taking its toll, and I was having to wait for him. We were walking more than we had planned. I began to wonder if the finish line would even still be set up by the time we made it to that point. I had dreamed about running this marathon for more years than I had even known Mark. Was I now facing a choice of staying with him, possibly not finishing the race, or going on without him and finishing alone? As we now approached Mile Marker 24, my thinking had become muddled, the result of running twenty-four miles with very little sleep the past few days, including none at all the night before.

My desire to complete that marathon had been building for twenty years. However, Mark's devotion to me, especially as I could see how the slower pace and heat was affecting him, touched me deeply. My dedication to him, and now my desire to finish with him by my side, was much stronger than my commitment to my marathon dream. However, I realized that whatever happened these last few miles, it was time to rededicate myself.

My effort to lose weight over the years was much like attempting to climb a tall ladder. In fact, I kept picturing myself standing at the foot of this huge ladder, squinting up toward the top, knowing my weight-loss goal was up there but unable as yet to see it. The ground was my comfort zone. Although I would tell myself that I would much rather be at the top, or at least *trying* to get there, the truth is I felt safer on the ground. Yet, I desperately wanted to reach the top, and so I would try again. But after mounting a few rungs, I would slip and fall. Getting back up, I would brush myself off and try again. I might get a little further this time, and then something would happen to knock me off once more. Many times the fall would hurt; other times it was as if being back on the ground was a welcome relief. I was amazed at how often I would wobble and fall. Sometimes I didn't get good enough footing; other times I would meet up with some obstacle that would come along, and since my grasp on the ladder was not strong enough to withstand the force, I would tumble to the ground. I knew that I needed to cling much more firmly to the rungs if I was going to ever succeed. However, I tired of trying to pull myself up, and I would often wonder why I was even trying to climb that stupid ladder. What was the use? And it would happen again and again and *again*.

During the years I struggled with morbid obesity, I found keeping a journal extremely helpful. It enabled me to sort through the emotions of why I ate and identify those emotions and situations where I felt compelled to eat more than I should. Remembering those times also helped me feel recommitted, as I replaced bad habits with good ones.

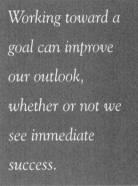

Working toward a goal can improve our outlook, whether or not we see immediate success.

Just a few months after Hillary was born, two friends, who each wanted to lose about ten pounds, invited me to go walking with them in the mornings. I was excited and flattered, and I really wanted to do it—until I started thinking about what that would mean. I was horrified to imagine what I would look like out there, especially next to them, with my hips swaying back and forth all over the road. Actually, it wasn't just my hips. My arms, stomach, rear end—the whole package—totally jiggled when I walked. I wondered if I would even be able to keep up with them without huffing and puffing myself to death. Nevertheless, I really wanted to go. I thought if I exercised enough on our treadmill inside, I could feel more comfortable being outside there with them.

But in the end I chickened out. I was nursing Hillary at the time, and it was easy to rationalize that I needed to be with her in the mornings. That may have been true early on in her life and at various times throughout the following months, but it was really just an excuse not to go with them. I've since thought that had I wanted to go with them badly enough, I would have found a way. It was a wonderful opportunity that I missed, and looking back, I wish I had given it a try.

That was only one of the times I dodged having to face the tremendous uphill battle of losing that much weight. It was an overwhelming, daunting task. If asked at that time to describe how I felt about my ability to shed those pounds, the best word would have been *hopeless*. There were other areas in my life where I felt satisfied and even fulfilled. I had a wonderful husband and children, and I loved my family. I was strengthened by my religious beliefs. Mark had a great job, and although there wasn't much extra, we had enough money to get by. Nevertheless, the way I felt about my weight seemed to overshadow and affect so many other areas in my life. I often hoped I could lose weight, but I also despaired of ever being able to really do it. Looking back, I realize that as long as *hopeless* and *despair* were part of my vocabulary in describing what needed to be done, I was not going to be successful. Feeling optimistic about my endeavor and having faith that I could do it, as incredibly difficult as it seemed, was crucial to my success.

I smile when I think about my visits to the dentist. The six month interval between checkups provided a gauge for me to monitor my weight. When I would go into the office, I would feel depressed that I had not lost any weight since the previous cleaning. Quite often, in fact, there would be a weight gain. Then, as I would leave the office, holding my toothbrush and floss in my hefty little hand (except for the time when the hygienist didn't *give* me a toothbrush), I would think, "Okay, the *next* time I go in there, I'm going to be thin! Or at least not quite as heavy! If I lose a mere ten pounds each month, I'll be sixty pounds lighter the next time he sees these teeth!" Then six more months would roll around, and so would I.

I continued to attempt to climb the slippery weight-loss ladder, climbing a few rungs, then being hurled back to the ground. Autumn of 2000 was just such a time. I had been exercising faithfully for almost four weeks, and I was trying to eat more healthy food and get more rest. I had definitely begun yet another ascent up the ladder. I was thrilled to see that I had even made it quite a ways. I felt healthier. There were also changes on the scale, and I noticed a difference in how my clothes fit. Then one morning I began to feel as if I were coming down with the flu. After a few days, I went to the doctor and discovered I had pneumonia. I was sick for weeks, too weak to even fix meals or do the laundry. My angel mother came down and helped me for a few days, and thoughtful friends and neighbors brought in meals and helped with the children. I had not been that sick for a long time. Even though I felt lousy, I was overjoyed to lose seven pounds. I thought for sure I would lose more, but I was also lying around all day. As soon as I started feeling better and eating again, the weight flew back on even quicker than it had come off. I gained back all seven pounds and found a few more as well. It is hard to describe how discouraged I felt. I had been trying so diligently! It was a huge setback for me.

As I continued to recuperate, still feeble and coughing all day and night, my weight continued to rise. Disheartened, I had no desire to exercise. For a few months, it was hard to shake the discouragement. I began to pray even more earnestly. I wanted God to know I was trying, harder than I ever had before. I also offered prayers of gratitude for the change of heart that I had before I became so sick. I wanted to get better. I wanted so desperately to win this weighty conflict. I also prayed for understanding. I wanted to know what my Heavenly Father was trying to teach me.

As I have thought about this experience and so many other

setbacks in my attempts to lose weight, I believe that most of the time my resolve to climb back up that ladder became even stronger each time I fell. How grateful I am for that strength, which helped me to ultimately reach the top of the ladder.

Finally, I began my weight-loss crusade in earnest soon after Eric was born. My commitment level was high. I was weighing in each week, keeping careful track of my food intake, drinking plenty of water, and eating healthier food. I was also exercising, thinking ahead, planning my meals, and organizing my time better. During this time of weight loss, however, I experienced many setbacks. There were times I fell back into familiar patterns of eating. I would have to yank myself out of those old behaviors by reminding myself how much more exhilarated I felt when I was living a healthier life.

I decided it didn't do much good to beat myself up unduly if I occasionally fell off the wagon. The important thing was to get up and climb back on. The effects of exercise and rejuvenation were powerful, especially if I had been particularly indulgent with my eating. On some occasions when we ate at a restaurant, I would order something that I later wished I hadn't. For years, I had ordered whatever I wanted, without seriously considering the consequences. But as I began ordering healthier choices on a more regular basis, which was something I never thought I would or could do for an extended period of time, I actually began to favor the better choices. It became easier to eat healthier. The harder I tried, the easier it became, and the better I felt.

There were times when after a week of dutifully exercising, drinking plenty of water, writing down everything I ate, and eating the right foods, I would still gain weight. That was discouraging, but I also had weeks where I had not worked as hard, and

I would lose a pound or two. The important thing was that there was a definite, downward trend in the amount I weighed.

Although it was quite difficult at times, I tried not to let the numbers on the scale dictate my attitude. I discovered that if I was consistently trying to do the right thing, the results followed. That helped tremendously.

Many of the setbacks I experienced while attempting to lose weight occurred when I did not plan very well. For example, one evening, I knew our family was going to have pizza for dinner. I had planned to eat a big salad before picking up the pizza, so I would not be tempted to eat as much. I ended up not making time to fix the salad, and we had dinner later than we had intended. I felt famished by the time we finally sat down to eat, and although I

The underlying cause of the problem (for example, turning to food to deal with life's ups and downs) can be more difficult to address than the symptoms of the problem (eating too much).

told myself I would only have one slice of pizza and then fix the salad, my ravaging hunger took over, and I ate much more that night than I should have. Obviously, that can't happen too often if someone is going to succeed at trying to lose weight.

In trying to analyze what finally made a difference and what kept me going this last time and why I was finally able to succeed, this is what I have discovered.

Each of those countless times that I started an exercise and/or eating program, it would last for a time and then I'd be right back to where I was before. For thirteen years I had felt as though I could "do it myself," that I didn't need to pay anyone for the privilege of stepping on their scale and be humiliated or have someone tell me I was eating too many of the wrong things and not enough of the right things. I *knew* which foods were healthy and which were not. I had learned that consuming more calories than I was expending would cause weight gain. Some say that if one *knows* all that, why continue in these self-defeating behaviors, gaining weight and continuing to be heavy? One of the keys to my success was surrendering to the weekly weigh-in—having to report and be accountable to someone else. In my case, I found that I *couldn't* "do it myself."

For many years, I thought that if I succeeded in losing weight, most of my problems would somehow go away. Although I had certainly heard otherwise, I continued to think that would be the scenario. After losing forty pounds, I recorded: "Although I still feel like the same person I was forty pounds ago, I now look at life differently. My problems have not gone away. However, I am able to meet challenges more easily, because I feel more confident in my ability to tackle difficulties. Because I am experiencing success in this area, which had seemed impossible for so long, I know I can succeed in other areas as well. Feeling more in control of myself has given me a sense of self-mastery. This is such a battle for me. However, it is incredible to realize that my resistance to temptation can be stronger than my appetite for food."

About nine months and eighty pounds into my weight loss, I experienced another incredible yet simple realization. It was on a morning when I looked out the window to a familiar sight. My neighbor and friend Lisa was taking her dog, Shiloh, out for a walk. Shiloh was a lucky beagle. She got a few walks each day, and it was fun to watch her excitement as she ventured out on her daily treks. As I watched them this particular day, I thought about Lisa. She had made a defining decision in her life. Rain or shine, day after day, she and Shiloh walked. Lisa also taught a spinning class a few mornings each week, and she and her husband occasionally ran together as well. I admired the fact that she stayed so active. By now I had been doing something similar for almost a year. For some reason, that day, as I watched Lisa, realizing what a priority exercise had become in her life, it hit me like a ton of bricks. In order for me to keep up this weight loss and overall feeling of good health, I would need to also make this a permanent decision, and continue some form of exercise for the rest of my life! Although I had always sort of known that, it hit home that particular day, and for a few days afterward, it was as if a new awareness had been born. This was *not* just a program that would end when I had met my weight goal. *This was a new lifestyle;* and one that I would need to continue as long as I wanted to maintain a wonderful feeling of fitness. Although I enjoyed exercise, many days it was still difficult to make myself get out. I sometimes felt too tired, although I still did it. Other times, it seemed quite complicated to schedule an exercise session and I would have to do some creative figuring to get in a workout. It certainly was not easy. However, reminding myself that I had made a life decision to exercise consistently was essential as I continued to take one step at a time.

> *Challenge the "I can do it myself" mentality.*

There were times, particularly when I missed my two babies, when I longed for the comfort food had given me. One of those times was the fall of 2001, when I suffered a big-time setback. When all the children were at school that first day, including Hillary in preschool, I came home to an empty house. Ordinarily I would have been excited to come home and have a few hours to myself. It was a luxury I had not often enjoyed over the previous fifteen years. However, what I really wanted was to come back home and take care of a new baby. It was a very difficult time for me. It was also a time, because of the terrorist attack on September 11, that the whole world seemed to be spinning out of control. There were days that autumn where I felt unsettled and numb; I felt sorrow, anger, and helplessness. I thought of how little children expressed emotions such as these. I had seen my children throw enough tantrums, including quite a few in public, so I was very familiar with how it was done. There were times when I, too, wanted to throw myself on the floor and kick my feet as hard as I could. I wanted to scream, pound my fists, and sob.

During this setback, I turned again to food for the comfort it provided. I desperately wanted my baby, and I felt sorry for myself. And, along with much of the nation, I was often glued to the news on TV when I should have been out walking.

It was time for a little internal dialogue. I thought about all I had done the past six months. I had been so careful and worked so hard. There was a tiny bit of light coming through the long, seemingly endless tunnel. After all these years, I was at last feeling as though the "real me" was emerging from this massive body. Now what was I doing? Was I really going to destroy all my hard work?

Frequent pep talks such as these helped me to rededicate myself to my goals.

I had to work hard to get back on track that fall. It was a chance for rededication. During such a difficult time, it was vital for me to focus on the positive elements and the new habits I had embedded in my lifestyle. Although I was still getting used to them, I wanted them to be part of my everyday life.

With Halloween just around the corner, I told myself that no matter how good a deal I could get on candy, my major downfall, I would not buy any more big packages of Halloween candy—at least no earlier than the day before Halloween. Even then, I hoped I would be strong enough to buy the stuff I did not like too well, so I wouldn't be tempted to eat it. That, of course, narrowed the choices quite a bit.

I seemed to be a slow learner at times because a few months later, just after Christmas, I bought some candy that had been marked down to next to nothing. It's hard to pass up a great deal! It was a big mistake, though, because I could not seem to stay away from it as I dealt with everyday challenges, and as I stayed up the next few nights, taking care of sick children, seeking for solace in late-night eating. I felt horrible after I indulged—disgusted and guilty—the old, familiar feelings I had always experienced whenever I lost control of my eating. Times like these still occurred occasionally, but I noticed they were happening a lot less frequently. Was I really on my way?

A year later, I realized how far I'd come. It was just after Christmas 2002, and I was in the grocery store, walking past cart after cart full of delicious leftover Christmas candy, all at marked-down prices. I remembered how I had felt the previous year, after giving in to my cravings, and I took great joy in the fact that this year I was able to walk right by them. I felt so empowered! I even smiled and asked the checker if he wouldn't mind hurrying up and selling all that candy, so it would be gone the next time I came in. He just grinned.

One motivation for me was that I continued to think about running the *Deseret News* Marathon the following summer. I recorded that fall, nine months before the race: "My big dream is to run in the marathon next summer. I want so badly to do it.

To just finish it! Today I am surer than ever before that I want to do it and that I *can* do it!" Looking forward to that goal helped me to stay on track.

Through the setbacks and pitfalls there certainly have been moments of triumph. One night I had been talking to Mark about some projects he was developing at work, and he was feeling particularly anxious about them. As he explained his concerns to me, I became anxious, too. A few nights later, when everyone was in bed, I lay awake thinking and becoming increasingly concerned about job security, medical bills, as well as other issues that seemed bigger and more serious at nighttime than in the light of day. I was stressed, I wanted to eat, and somehow felt like I deserved to eat. In no way was I feeling hungry, but my old familiar enemy was rearing his ugly head, and I thought eating would make me feel better. I lay there and thought about what I could go snack on.

There had been countless other nights over the years when I had indulged in late-night binges. The difference now was that I was *really* on my way in my weight-loss journey. Did I want to sabotage that? I had another little internal dialogue, telling myself how senseless it would be to eat anything, especially that late at night, knowing I had already eaten all the food I needed that day. I recognized that it would be purely emotional eating. I was surprised how strong that unhealthy coping skill *still* was! It had actually been a few months since I had felt such a strong desire to eat for emotional reasons.

I reminded myself, in this little inner discussion, that I had just weighed in that day and had a significant weight loss, and I had been doing so well that week. "Didn't that matter?" I asked myself. I decided that no, it didn't, and I was bound and determined to go find something to eat. I could hear a few of the children still awake, and I wanted to wait until they were asleep to begin my eating frenzy. Although the desire to indulge was still intense, I prayed for strength, as I did quite often.

My prayers were answered, once again in my best interest. The next thing I realized was the morning sun coming through the window. I had fallen asleep while waiting to begin my food fiesta. I awoke feeling rested and ready to run. I had a great workout that day! I knew I would not have had the same results if I had surrendered to the impulse to over-indulge.

> *In continually rededicating ourselves to our goal, we will recognize that a lifestyle is actually a life journey, not a destination.*

As I continued to experience setbacks and triumphs, I began to think that this might be somewhat of a pattern for the rest of my life. That night, my setback seemed to be that I was determined, no matter what, to eat my troubles away once again. The triumph came when it did not happen. Although I seemed dead-set on getting up and eating, I *was* going to wait a few minutes until the kids went to sleep. That took a little determination and self-control, didn't it? I had to remind myself that the success was due to *some* effort on my behalf, although I attributed the triumph of that night to the power of heartfelt prayer. I continued to recognize this tremendous power. I was also recognizing that I was becoming stronger at resisting temptation. However, since I had been such an emotional eater for so long, I knew that it would take time to overcome this habit. Nevertheless, I felt as if I had jumped over an enormous hurdle that night. I also knew I had not jumped over it alone. I was grateful for the heavenly help I received.

In attending one of Hillary's dance recitals, I was once again impressed by how freely children express their emotions. Watching these darling little girls move around the stage to the music, it was evident that they were feeling *pure joy*. They whirled around, lifting their little legs, pointing their toes, stretching their arms out, and shaking their bouncy curls as they danced. It didn't seem to matter if they had stout little stomachs or chubby thighs; they were just happy to be there. It was total happiness. I thought that quite often, as I rededicated myself, I felt just like these small dancers. In times of rejuvenation, I felt like twirling around and leaping for joy. Although that is somewhat of a scary visual, what an incredible feeling! I discovered that as I experienced more triumphs, I experienced fewer setbacks. I felt at peace knowing that if I persisted, in the end, I would come out a winner!

> *We can enjoy the empowerment of being able to control urges.*

In the aftermath of my weight loss, I also have enjoyed going to get my teeth cleaned. How thrilling it was, in preparing for my first marathon, to run a half-marathon down beautiful Provo Canyon. And who should be running the same race but my dentist! Now I look forward to visiting with him about training runs, instead of lamenting at how much more I fill up his examination chair!

We were just a few miles from the finish line. We were walking now more than running, and Mark was encouraging me to go on ahead. He still felt terrible, and I did not want to leave him. I knew there were those who, even though I had faltered and stumbled my way through weight loss, had not given up on me. Mark was my biggest cheerleader. He

had stuck with me, literally through thick and thin, and loved me regardless of how much I weighed. While we walked along, I was so grateful for the love and support he had offered through the years. He had trained for this marathon with me, an incredible act of love in and of itself, and he had stayed with me through the entire race. In spite of the distress he was feeling, he had even carried my bottle of Gatorade all the way down Emigration Canyon.

There was no way I was giving up on him. We were almost there. We would finish together!

CHAPTER ELEVEN

The Marathon Miracle

Most of the marathoners had already finished the race. Mark and I still had two miles to go. Police officers rode by on their shiny motorcycles and told us that the barricades used to aid the runners would now be moved to allow traffic to flow once again. Instead of having a police escort through the intersections, we were now to obey the traffic signals. The route weaved through the streets of downtown Salt Lake City and was difficult to follow, especially with the barricades now removed. I was glad I had studied the map beforehand and had memorized the course. I felt more mentally prepared than physically ready for this race. Running this marathon had been in most of my waking thoughts the past few months. I reflected back on all the time and effort I had spent in pursuit of this goal.

Their faces told it all. It was the summer of 1978, and even through my seventeen-year-old eyes, I could see clearly. Joy, pain, anticipation, relief—it was all there. They had been running three, four, some even five hours that morning. I was with Marie and Joni, two of my best friends, helping at the Salt Lake City *Deseret News* Marathon. Marie's parents were helping to organize the race, and they had involved us in the volunteer effort. We helped the athletes cross the finish line, mostly by directing them to the water and first-aid tables but occasionally lending a shoulder to lean on as we helped them find some relief. Most of them looked incredibly triumphant. Many were hurting. Still others appeared to wonder, *What in the world was I thinking?* The faces I remember most were those full of victory and accomplishment.

I thought about the difficulty of this marathon, including the heat, the many hills, and the high altitude. Originating in 1970 and commemorating the arrival of the Mormon pioneers on July 24, 1847, the course includes the same canyon the pioneers used as they entered the Salt Lake Valley.

As I shared that day with the runners, I was so impressed by it all that I too wanted to experience this marathon for myself. My dream was born.

Growing up, I was not an avid runner. The closest I came to running was when the junior high school coaches recruited me to be on the track team. It was not my running skills they were after, however; it was my ability to throw a ball. The "Basketball Throw" and the "Softball Throw," equivalents of the shot put, were the only two events in which I participated. Although I enjoyed being part of the team, those events were not ones I was very excited about doing. I was like most other girls my age, preferring to show my femininity instead of how far I could hurl a ball. Fortunately, that mentality seems to have changed over the years. Now, the strength and ability to throw long distance is something of which to be proud.

It wasn't until after I graduated from high school that I really got into running. My desire to run the July 24th marathon continued, and one year, while I was in college, I even began training. But I was also a member of a university choir, and we had an opportunity to go to Europe that summer. The two weeks we would be gone came during a critical training period, and I knew I would not be able to take the time for long training runs. I also did not want to pass up such a wonderful travel experience. So I chose to go to Europe. Most summers after that, I was either pregnant, nursing a baby, and/or living outside Utah. I always seemed to have an excuse, valid or not, as to why it wasn't possible for me to train for the race. But Mark and I often talked about running that marathon together. My dream lived on.

When I was at my heaviest, however, and considered that dream, a comparison frequently came to mind. While we were living in Texas, my children loved to pick dandelions and blow the countless tiny seeds into the air. We also experienced incredible winds when hurricanes would pound the Gulf of Mexico. Even at our home, 145 miles inland, the wind was very powerful. Trying to retrieve a dandelion full of delicate little seeds during a hurricane seemed an utterly impossible task. I felt the same way about the reality of losing weight and running a marathon—that it was an impossibility, and a discouraging one at that.

One year, Mark and his friend Gerry decided to run the *Deseret News* Marathon. I watched the two men train, and it seemed like such an exciting challenge. I was thrilled for Mark.

It was also painful for me, though, because I wanted so badly to be doing it, too. I felt powerless and full of excuses. I must have asked myself a million times why I could not just *do* it. If I really wanted to run a marathon so much, why couldn't I buckle down, lose weight, and begin training?

When the day of the big race came, I took our children down to meet Mark and Gerry at "Mile Marker 19," at the mouth of Emigration Canyon, bringing a supply of Gatorade and Ibuprofen. There was an area there, just off the

> *Dreams can be achieved when they are turned into goals.*

side of the road, where we could stand and watch the runners come by. Mark had informed me the approximate time he thought they would make it to that point.

We waited with other well-wishers, clapping and shouting words of encouragement as each runner passed. I felt a huge lump in my throat as I watched these marathoners, young and old. It was inspiring to realize they had been running three hours already and to watch the effort they were making. Some smiled and waved as they ran past. Others wore more serious expressions, totally focused on the task at hand or lost in their personal agony.

Then something happened that absolutely stunned me. One of the runners, a man about fifty years of age, came by. As he passed our little cheering section, he looked right at me and called out, "You should be out here!" I quickly glanced around. *Is he really talking to me?* It struck me at first that he must have meant that he was feeling so great that he wanted the whole lot of us to be out there, running with him. But he had looked right into my eyes, not at the crowd. He had singled *me* out of the group. Why would he say that? It pierced my soul. My children looked up at me, puzzled. It took us all by surprise. I noticed that no one else in our little cheerleading cluster came close to being as heavy as I was. There was not a whole lot of reason to wonder why he singled me out. I was hoping none of the strangers around me had heard his comment, but I was sure some had. I did not know this man; I had never seen him before in my life. Was he delirious? Although I tried to rationalize his behavior, I felt devastatingly numb, and terribly humiliated.

Mark and Gerry came soon after that, and although we cheered and clapped for them, too, I was still feeling rather embarrassed. We took some pictures, and they were off for the last leg of the marathon. The children and I drove to the finish line and watched as they triumphantly ran across. I also watched for the man who had spoken to me, secretly wanting to trip him, but ready to attempt to hide if I saw him. But I never saw him again. I wondered if it had all just been an illusion; but I knew better. I also wondered why his challenge affected me so much. Perhaps because I wanted so badly to be out there, living my dream. He had rubbed salt in the wound. And the longer I thought about it, the ruder his comment seemed. Just because he had been running for more than three hours, did that entitle him to say anything he wanted to the spectators?

Or was he bringing me a message? Was he confirming what I already knew? That I really did need to be out there, running that marathon? What he said to me also reinforced something I had experienced over the years. As strange as it sounds, weighing as much as I did, I did not feel part of "the real world." My real, authentic self was obscured by my size, and it was as if I almost wasn't even a member of the human race. I also felt as if

I was being prevented from fully rising to the potential that was in me. It was a frustrating and awful feeling.

Even though after that difficult run Mark said he would "never do it again," he did run it a few years later. He vowed again that it would be his last marathon. It is a tough run! Both times, as he trained for the *Deseret News* Marathon, as well as when he ran the St. George Marathon, I admired his incredible determination. I also envied the immense satisfaction he obviously experienced when he finished the race and had reached his goal. I wanted so badly to be part of it. Not only did I want to experience running a marathon with *him*, I wanted to run it for *myself* as well.

Then came the summer of 2001. I once again watched as Mark and our son Nick ran that day, this time completing the 10K, held the same morning and following the last 6.2 miles of the *Deseret News* Marathon route. I also paid particular attention to the marathoners. I noticed two familiar runners. They lived near my home, and I would often see them out training while I was on my walks. They were elite runners, members of what I thought of as "running royalty," and it was an inspiring thing to watch their strength and stride as they would fly by me. Some days I almost felt as though I should bow down as they passed.

As my two neighbors crossed the finish line that day, one of them promptly threw up. A few more people came in, and I could see that they were all exhausted and some of them even delirious. It was a bit scary watching them. I thought about the serious consequences that could result from running such a long distance. I still wanted to do it, although I realized that accomplishing this feat would be no small undertaking.

Each summer, when I would tell myself that "next year"

would be my year to run that marathon, I realized I was mostly saying it to keep my dream alive. However, that summer of 2001 was different. I had succeeded in losing forty pounds. I considered my situation. By this time next year, would I have lost enough additional weight, be in good enough shape and sufficiently trained to be able to complete the marathon? I already felt so much healthier! As I watched the runners, I wanted so much to be out there with them.

Something wonderful happened that day. I began to think my dream of running this marathon actually had a glimmer of hope of becoming a reality. It was that day that I finally began, after so many years, to turn my dream into an actual goal. I still was not sure whether I could really do it; after all, at that point, I had not even begun running yet. Did I still know how? There was also the issue of carrying around sixty extra pounds. They were not going to be easy or fun to get rid of. But now I realized more than ever just how badly I wanted to achieve my goal.

Something else was happening. The idea of completing the marathon was becoming more enticing than the immediate gratification I would get from eating.

One morning, soon after that, I tried running. To make sure no one would see me, I went early enough so it was still dark. I went only about ten paces before I had to stop. I laughed right out loud, imagining how in the world I thought I could run a whole 26.2 miles, if I could now only run ten steps! A few days later, while I was on another early morning walk, I tried running again. This time I went a few more paces. Each day after that, in the predawn darkness, I tried running. I began at the same starting point, and then made sure I went just a little further than I had the day before. I took it one step at a time.

Then one morning, Mark and I went on a walk, and he

encouraged me to run a little ways with him. We went farther than I had ever gone by myself. I was able to run about a quarter of a mile without stopping. I was ecstatic! A few months earlier I started out running ten paces, panting so hard I could barely breathe, and now I had worked up to running a quarter of a mile without stopping. It was a huge deal for me! It was incredible, though, to think how much farther I would have to go to even consider running a marathon. I would have to run just over one hundred more of those quarter miles to complete the marathon. Whoa.

> We must not allow self-consciousness to hold us back from doing what we really want to do.

I will always remember those early mornings when I began running, if only a little ways, for the first time in many years. Even though I started out going only a short distance, I felt as though I was almost flying. I was still quite overweight but somehow felt as light as a feather. It was invigorating to be out and running. Without those forty pounds I had hauled around for so long, I could actually move. I kept imagining what it would feel like with another sixty pounds gone. Nine months later, when they were finally gone, it was a thrilling sensation. It was an unbelievable feeling, to be able to move so much more freely.

One huge roadblock remained for me, however. I was very self-conscious about how I looked while walking fast or running. That image was something that had held me back for years and continued to have a hold on me. One day I recorded, "I am trying to run a little more, and with daylight coming earlier now, it is often light when I go out on my walks. However, I have not yet run past other people who are walking on the track, because they will see my big body bouncing all over the place! As a result, I stop and walk whenever I approach anyone, so I won't have to pass them. Sometimes the track is very crowded, so I do not run too much. It is still so embarrassing, thinking about my wiggly, jiggly behind. I see many women out walking or running who are quite fit. I pretty much jostle all over the track."

When I first began walking in the spring of 2001, soon after little Eric's birth, I was easily the biggest person out on that track, and I was extremely self-conscious about it. I had to tell myself repeatedly that it didn't really matter how I looked; I was out there to get some exercise and to feel better. I continued to lose weight, and one day I realized I was no longer the biggest person out there. I also discovered that when I saw people who were bigger than I was, I felt no inclination to ridicule or feel ashamed for them. In fact, I was thrilled for them; they were doing something for their health. Previously, I had been sure others wanted to laugh when they would see me. But now that I was starting to cross over to the other side of the hurdle, I wondered if most people didn't just feel the same way I did now—joy at the sight of people actually doing something about their weight problem.

I continued to run, pushing myself just a little farther each time. Then one night it happened. It was late that summer on a beautiful clear evening. I was feeling great and I decided I was going to run a mile. The sprinklers were running on the field around the track, and I did not even mind getting wet as I ran. This particular track was unusual in that it measured just short of a half mile in its circumference. I made it one time around, and I was amazed to find that I could still keep going without feeling too winded. As I ran that second lap, I reflected on those first, tentative ten paces that had so recently left me breathless and unable to go on. Being able to complete a marathon still seemed a million miles away, but realizing how far I had come these past few months, I was encouraged that I might actually be able to do it. When I neared the end of that second lap and realized I was actually going to make it a mile without stopping, it was such a thrill. And as I crossed the mile point, I didn't know whether to laugh or cry. It had been almost twenty years since I had run that far without stopping. It was hard to believe! Was I just dreaming? I was certainly ready to stop and rest at that point, but as I walked the short distance home, I was walking on air. I was elated!

The confidence I gained from the run that night was incredible. As I had so many times, I felt help from above. I also pictured my two little angels cheering me on. I seemed to be hearing, "Go, Mom—you can do it!" It was just one of many occasions that I felt as though I was truly running with angels.

It was about then that I finally realized that it did not matter WHAT anybody else thought of my fat bottom as it jiggled and rippled all over the track. I had truly been embarrassed by my big body, and when I would run past someone who was walking, I almost felt a need to turn around and apologize for what they had to look at as I bounced by. However, I worked hard to overcome that humiliation, and I knew that as I continued to exercise, I would feel better about myself and the shame would become less of an issue.

I realized also I would have to put my fears and doubts aside if I were going to go through with the marathon. I knew there would be plenty of people watching me, jiggle and all, and I would just have to get over that and stop placing such importance on what other people thought of me. Let them think what they wanted. I was out there—doing what I knew was good for my physical and emotional health.

Friends who encouraged me were truly earthly angels. My friend Kathleen was a huge support during my weight loss. I excitedly called her on my cell phone while I was on my way home from the meeting where I discovered I had lost fifty pounds. By the time I arrived, she had gathered some other friends and they met me, clapping and shouting, "Congratulations!" Their demonstration of support bolstered my determination to continue. What wonderful, encouraging women! It was a definite highlight. I felt that night there was no way I would give up my goal.

I continued to run. That Utah winter was rather mild, and I loved getting outside as much as I could. There were also days when I ran on the treadmill. I continued to think about the marathon. I downloaded a map of the course from the Internet and hung it in front of my treadmill, where I could easily see it while I ran. Because I was familiar with most of the course, I could picture each stretch of the route quite clearly. As I ran on the treadmill, and later that spring and summer as I ran outside, I envisioned myself running the course. I must have run that marathon a thousand times in my mind before I actually physically ran it.

I also hung a poster of Mount Everest on the wall in front of my treadmill. The caption was a declaration by Sir Edmund Hillary, one of my heroes. He stated, "It is not the mountains we conquer but ourselves." I often reflected on that quote as I trained, and I realized how this marathon was becoming much more to me than just a race. It was a symbol of overcoming what I used to think was virtually impossible.

The idea that I was conquering myself was an incentive that

helped push me to more weight loss. More and more, I was using self-control and substituting the satisfying feeling that came from taking better care of myself for the gratification I used to get from eating.

I found a few running books to be helpful. My friend Ruth, who was an avid runner, loaned me a book entitled *The Non-Runner's Marathon Trainer*, by David A. Whitsett, Forrest A. Dolgener, and Tanjala Mabon Kole. I still remember the day she brought it over to me. Her eyes sparkled as she described the rush she got from long-distance running. She seemed so excited for me and was very encouraging. Reading the book, I discovered that the authors had written it for people like me, who wanted to complete a marathon but who had little or no running experience. The book helped me understand what I could expect as I trained. It also contained comments from first-time marathon runners, as well as information on stretching, nutrition, and relaxation. It included a training schedule, which I posted on the refrigerator, where I could see it often. It helped remind me, especially when I was tempted to open the fridge more than I needed, of all the hard work I had put in. Every time I completed a training run, I highlighted that day and recorded where and how far I had gone. I was able to see my goal coming closer with each day of running.

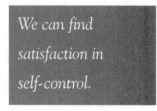

We can find satisfaction in self-control.

I also wrote out the phrase "I am a Marathoner!" and posted it right next to my training schedule. I taped the same words to the top of the bathroom mirror. Whenever I looked at my reflection, I would repeat the phrase aloud, so I could actually hear the words. It seemed so basic; but it helped to begin thinking of myself as a legitimate runner. It was exciting to think in those terms, and the idea especially helped on those days when I sure did not feel like one.

The training schedule I adopted was a sixteen-week program that assumed the person had already been running regularly. Each week I was to complete four runs—two short ones, one medium, and one long run. It measured mileage instead of time, which was good for me, because I was not a fast runner. The total mileage for the first week was fifteen miles. During the height of training, I would cover thirty-six miles a week. The longest single run I did was twenty miles. On the days when I did not run, I walked. Sunday was a welcome rest. I learned how important it was to take a break each week, especially between the medium and long runs, to give my body a chance to recover.

During this time, I gained an even better appreciation for the human body. I was continually amazed at how forgiving my body was of the years of abuse I had put it through with too much food and not enough exercise. As my conditioning improved and my stamina increased, I felt bad that I had spent so many years overweight and out of shape. Because of the poor choices I had made, I had missed out on a lot, but I was grateful to have learned from the past, and I was looking forward to the future.

Going through the training was quite an experience. There were days when I had to remind myself that I really wanted to do this. With five children and busy lives, I had to plan and prioritize my time to make sure I could get my runs. I also found the importance of getting enough sleep, drinking enough water, and eating wisely.

To reach my goal, I still needed to lose five pounds, but they refused to come off. I was frustrated by the stubbornness of the scale, particularly in light of how much I was running. I was also much hungrier, and I wondered if my body hadn't gone into starvation mode. I had read somewhere that training for a marathon is not an effective way to lose weight. It places too much demand on the body to expect weight loss as well as conditioning. Therefore, during the month just before the marathon, I stopped being concerned about trying to lose weight. I had already asked a lot from my body; in the previous fifteen months, it had ridded itself of one hundred pounds. I continued my training schedule and was quite careful about what and how much I ate, writing everything down. However, I ate to satisfy my hunger, requiring more food, especially before and after the long runs. During the few weeks following the marathon, those last five pounds came right off.

Occasionally during the training, I suffered overuse injuries. I knew I was pushing harder than I should have on some of my runs, but it was so invigorating, being able to move so freely without the burden of the extra hundred pounds I had been lugging around for all those years. I felt so light it was as if I were gliding through the air. But I learned to be careful and made certain to stretch before and especially after each workout.

One such injury occurred just eight weeks before the marathon. I was experiencing quite a bit of pain in my right foot and could barely walk. A few days earlier, I had run harder than I probably should have. Since the pain was becoming increasingly worse, I went to the doctor. I told him how important running this marathon was to me, and he arranged for me to have a bone scan. He wanted to rule out a stress fracture, which, because of the healing time, would have taken me out of training for the *Deseret News* Marathon. As Mark reminded me, there *were* other marathons. However, that year, I had my sights set on *that* one.

When the technician escorted me into the X-ray room, I immediately noticed the narrow table and the small doughnut-like hole in the machine that I would have to pass through. My heart began to race as the familiar anxious fear of *will I fit?* swept over me. When I climbed up on the table and lay down, I was amazed not to feel my body spilling over the sides. I actually cried for joy when the machine easily passed over me, without getting hung up on any stoutness. Even with all the pain I was experiencing in my foot and wondering if I would get to complete my training, I felt such exhilaration knowing I could actually fit through that machine, with even a little room to spare.

While lying there, trying to be still, I thought back to a time, a few years earlier, when I had gone to see the doctor about foot pain. That time it had been my excessive weight that was causing such stress on the arches of my feet and so much pain that I could barely walk. Tears now flowed freely as I felt an intense gratitude that I was not here this time because of my obesity.

Reading the X ray, the radiologist did not see a fracture but said there was a possibility of torn ligaments. He congratulated me on my weight loss, and smiling, said, "Pam, our bodies aren't made to run marathons!" However, I felt his encouragement to continue training. *This* body wanted to run a marathon! For the next two weeks, instead of running and walking, I rode my bike and swam, which put less stress on my foot and allowed it to heal sufficiently to continue and finally complete the training. I was determined to take good care of myself.

Throughout the training, I was able to draw parallels between pursuing a weight-loss program and preparing for a marathon. Participating in a marathon is not just about race day. It's actually mostly about everything leading up to that moment, including *months*, and sometimes *years*, of taking training runs, eating properly, getting enough rest, wearing the right shoes, caring for injuries, and making intense mental preparation. Weight loss is not just about reaching "that number" on the scale. It encompasses much more, including breaking old and forming new habits, eating nutritious food, getting enough sleep, providing more effective self-care, and developing a more positive mental attitude. Just as I had to discipline myself to get out of bed and on the road in pursuit of improved conditioning, I also had to discipline myself to avoid overeating or eating the wrong kinds of food. In my case, the incentive to achieve one goal provided the incentive to achieve the other. I was grateful beyond expression that I had given myself a chance to experience both.

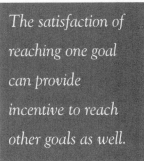

The satisfaction of reaching one goal can provide incentive to reach other goals as well.

Wow. After all this training, there I was, less than a mile from the finish line. I thought about how my pioneer ancestors must have felt after months of crossing the plains, and then, 155 years ago today, as they finally entered the Salt Lake Valley through the same canyon I had just run down. It was as if I, too, had experienced my own grueling expedition, totally changing my life and starting anew, just as they had, so long ago.

CHAPTER TWELVE

Running with Angels

We turned what would be the last corner, onto the final city block of the race. I looked toward the finish line. They *hadn't* taken it down yet! We had been running for over five and a half hours. That was certainly no record, but today, speed did not matter. What counted was that I was actually there, fulfilling my dream of running a marathon, savoring every sweet, sweaty drop of effort, celebrating everything and everyone that had helped me get there. I knew my family would be waiting. Even though my legs felt as if they had been on autopilot for the last mile and a half, they throbbed with every painful step. But now it was easy to ignore the pain. Here I was, with Mark, one hundred yards from the finish line of my first marathon. If I had previously questioned my ability to finish, I would worry no more. My dream was finally coming true! My feet plodded along, but I felt as if I were floating. I was soaring above the crowd, looking down and having one of those experiences that seemed so unreal it was actually dreamlike. I felt as though I was in a movie where everything was filmed in slow motion; I wasn't actually moving very fast anyway, but every stride, every difficult lift of my rubbery legs, every labored arm swing, even the cheering spectators, all seemed to move in a surreal slow motion. A few miles back I had felt intense, stiffening pain, and yet although my entire body ached, I was glad not to feel that particular pain anymore. The grimace that had contorted my face was now softening to hot, dry tears. My parched throat was quickly filling with a huge lump, making it difficult to breathe. I could not speak. It was as if I were being lifted up and carried, high above the crowd, floating my way to that finish line I had dreamed of count-less times.

So this is what it feels like! I had only seen it in their faces from behind the bright orange barricades; now I was actually a participant, a marathoner, experiencing the final stretch. It was still difficult to believe I was really within grasp of the finish line. I thought I saw some of the spectators wiping their eyes. I wasn't sure if they were happy for us or if they just felt incredibly sorry for us. A sense of euphoric accom-plishment swept over me, similar to what I had felt at the birth of my children.

This, too, had truly been a partnership with God. He had been my running companion and my training partner, not just in training for the marathon, but in helping me through the struggles of the past thirteen years. And I recognized His voice that had cheered me throughout this amazing fifteen-month marathon of weight loss and training. Yes, I had learned some incredible lessons not only during this time, but since Emily's death as well. It certainly felt as if my little heavenly angels, my arm-waving, pom-pom swinging celestial children had been there, cheering me on through my stumbles, my hit-the-wall times, my episodes of despair, and the occasions when I felt as if my heart would break. I knew they were near, cheering with me during months of weight loss, as well as during and after many lengthy training runs. I felt heavenly help during visits to doctors, unknowing moments of concern, as well as on joyful occasions. I realized that God was in charge, and He knew me, and was totally aware of my situation. I felt encouraged during the long days, weeks, and months of slowly, painfully turning my bad habits into better, healthier ones. I felt my little angels near during all of those times. And I certainly felt them here, today, their arms woven through mine, pulling me toward the finish line.

Nick and his friend, who had run the 10K race, now ducked under the barrier and ran with us during the last fifty-yard stretch. I looked over and saw my parents with huge smiles on their faces. Tears of joy (and concern!) streamed down my mother's cheeks. Seeing her opened up the floodgate in my own eyes, although there was not a whole lot of water left in the reservoir. Dad was snapping more photos, and our other children were shouting and cheering. Standing next to my parents were Mark's parents and his sister, Lisa, cheering and waving. I saw Jill, my sweet, devoted sister who I still couldn't believe had flown all the way from Boston to be there. She had the video camera going. It was all so overwhelming. I looked up toward the heavens. My amazement that I was finally here was now giving way to inexpressible thankfulness. I was overcome with a feeling of gratitude to my Father in Heaven, who had made all of this possible. Gratitude also to my heavenly angels, who I had felt were always near. And gratitude as well to all the earthly angels, who had shown so much love and encouragement and who had not given up on me. I knew I could not have come this far without them.

I reached down and patted my "list" one more time, which was still riding in the small pocket of my running shorts. It held the names of those to whom I had "dedicated" each

Embracing love and support from others will help us in whichever life race we run!

of the twenty-six miles. By now, the paper was moist and tattered and the writing smeared. Many times during this exhilarating run, I had pulled it out to review who was next on the list. Mark and I talked about each of those people as we ran together, reminiscing about the ways they were a significant part of our lives. The first half of the race belonged to our family members—our children, including Emily and Eric, our parents and siblings. My sweet ninety-seven-year-old Grandmother LeOra got mile number three. The last half we dedicated to friends who had supported us along the way. I managed a smile when I thought about the posters some of my friends had made, saying things like "You go, girl!" and "Good Luck!" Yesterday they had staked them right in the middle of our front yard with balloons all around, held down by bottles of water. My love and gratitude for all of them had grown during the past twenty-six miles.

I dedicated mile twenty-five to my beloved Mark, beside me all the way. Throughout the run, I had thought about his love and devotion to me. Together we had gone through dark valleys and over bright mountaintops, through storm and sunshine. He had shown sensitivity as we mourned the loss of our children, discussed and prayed endlessly for the health of our daughters, endured the many long years of his education, and as we continued simply trying to raise our family in a world of turmoil. He was at the same time, a rock and a tender, loving husband and father. His sense of humor had kept our trials in perspective all these years, and had, most of the time, kept me laughing.

Mark had loved me no matter what I weighed. So many times I had entered a "weight-loss marathon," only to quit early in the race. Yet his support had never wavered during all of my attempts, and I appreciated his kindness and patience more than I can say. This time I had hung on for dear life, with Mark by my side—and the finish line was finally in sight!

I dedicated the last mile to me. For many years, I had been so down on myself, and now it was time to celebrate this huge accomplishment. However, as I tried to think about what I had brought to the party, I realized that I could not have made it without the help of my heavenly and earthly angels. As I ran the last fifty yards, I wept as I realized that just over a hundred pounds ago I was able to run only ten steps before I became so winded I had to stop. And today I had run 26.2 miles. Dreams *do* come true!

Wearily yet triumphantly, I raised my arms, mostly because that is how I had pictured coming across the finish line. Clutching Mark's hand, we crossed together. A volunteer hung the gold "finisher" medal around our necks. A feeling of euphoria swept through every tired bone and aching muscle in my body. After Mark and I gave each other a victory hug, our family rushed over to share in our celebration. By this time, since there were fewer runners coming in, spectators were allowed inside the barricades. I knew I should stop and stretch; but the welcomed hugs and cheers kept coming.

I knew that today was a day I would remember my entire life. There may or may not be more marathons in my future, but certainly, I was determined that I would always make time for exercise. I had learned the importance of the now recognized value of loving myself enough to take better care of my body, as well as my spirit. More than anything, I knew the importance and blessing of eternal families.

I had also come to understand that the accomplishment of anything significant we try to do in our lives is like running a marathon. It takes tremendous commitment, valiant effort, and a degree of patience. Everyone faces challenges. Mine happened to have included my weight, the loss of children, and having to cope with our children's health issues. Our trials will continue throughout our lives. But we cannot give up. Even if we stumble and fall, we need to pick ourselves back up and keep running. We may not win the race, but speed does not matter. What matters is that we keep going, forging ahead, enjoying the journey, recognizing and feeling grateful for the divine and earthly help we receive along the way, and ultimately finishing the course. We can overcome. We *will* triumph. We are running with angels.

Afterword

by Mark H. Hansen

When Pam told me that she wanted to include an afterword, I suggested that she let me write it. I persuaded her by reasoning that as her husband, I could say things that she might be uncomfortable saying, although she has already addressed some very uncomfortable issues in the book. She was kind enough to let me do it.

I suspect that many readers are wondering at this point if she has kept the weight off. The answer is, yes she has. The complete unvarnished truth is that she must still be careful about her eating and exercising. She has often remarked that she knows this will be a lifelong struggle.

One of the things that I find most compelling about Pam's story is that she is an ordinary person—an ordinary person who has done something extraordinary. She didn't become obese overnight, and she didn't lose the weight overnight either. Both processes, gaining and losing, occurred a day, an hour, a minute, even a decision at a time. The remarkable thing about her accomplishment is that she was finally able to consistently make those little decisions to eat more wisely and exercise more regularly. I watched as she summoned inspiring willpower to stick with her plan. As I recall the events of the past three years, I am amazed by how the small, seemingly insignificant, decisions we make can influence our lives so profoundly.

Another thing readers should know about is Pam's motivation in sharing her story. Her desire has been to help others who may be facing similar challenges. She has repeatedly said that there were so many points in her journey when she would have loved to hear from someone else who had faced and had overcome some of the same challenges. She has vacillated back and forth many times between not wanting to share some embarrassing details of her life and wanting to help others. She has also wanted to avoid any perception that she is bragging about her accomplishment. Pam understands that some readers will say, "If the problem was that bad, why didn't she just stop eating so much?" She also understands that there are many out there who will identify with the difficulty of the struggle.

Pam has continued to exercise regularly. She has gone on to run another marathon. Her second was the St. George Marathon. She trained and ran with two of her girlfriends. One of the friends was running the marathon to celebrate her fiftieth birthday. Full disclosure requires me to admit that Pam's time improved by fifty-two minutes when she ran with her friends. During the *Deseret News* Marathon that Pam describes in the book, she waited on me through the last four miles. I broke down physically, and I had to walk during most of the last four miles. I encouraged Pam to go on without me, but she refused. In contrast, she told me how her girlfriends had played little games and told stories throughout the marathon to make it more fun. At about mile eighteen of that second marathon, one of her friends said, "Let's all name a body part that doesn't hurt yet." The friend quickly offered up "earlobes" as the only part that didn't hurt.

Pam and I now walk together several mornings a week. This has proven to be one of the most beneficial aspects of Pam's modified lifestyle. The conversations during those walks have brought us closer together as a couple. We are able to discuss things that would be difficult to discuss in other settings. Life's struggles, and there have been several significant ones since those described in the book, seem to be more easily handled when we are able to discuss them so freely and so frequently. Early morning walks with a close loved one, or sometimes all alone, are very therapeutic—both physically and psychologically.

There is a humorous epilogue to one of the stories in the book. Pam discovered through a series of conversations that the man who told her that she should be out there running a marathon (page 185) is actually one of our friends and neighbors. Hawk and Cheryl Harper own a running store in Orem, Utah. Pam mentions the running lesson that Hawk gave her in Chapter 9. Hawk and Cheryl have run many marathons. Cheryl is a world-class runner, having won the women's division of several marathons. Their children are also accomplished runners. As Pam began training for her first marathon she would occasionally go into their running store for shoes and clothing. Hawk always looked familiar to Pam, as if she had seen him somewhere before.

One day they told Pam about the time that Hawk had dropped out of the *Deseret News* Marathon. With about six miles left to go, Hawk realized that he was within a block of their hotel at the University of Utah's Research Park. He remembered the hot tub and a box of doughnuts that was waiting in the room. Hawk decided he had had enough running that day, so he left the course and ran to the hotel. In another conversation, Hawk told Pam that Cheryl often tells him that he talks too much to people along the routes of the marathons he runs. Pam began to wonder if Hawk could have been the man that told her she should be out there running a marathon. Pam's curiosity worked on her until she summoned the nerve to ask Cheryl and Hawk which year it was that Hawk had left the course. Well, as you might expect, it was 1997, the same year that the man had made the comment to Pam. She then told Hawk what the man had said and asked if he could have been the man who made such a comment. He smiled and said that it was very likely. He offered a quick apology when he realized that the comment might have been offensive. He certainly didn't intend to be cruel. You'll recall that Pam never saw that man at the finish area that year. Apparently he was enjoying the hot tub and doughnuts at his hotel. How ironic that a few years later the same man was giving Pam running tips.

Another humorous, yet telling, anecdote involves the toothbrush that Pam didn't get at the dentist's office (Chapter 6). Pam visited the dentist's office during the writing of the book. She mentioned to the hygienist that she had included the story about the time that she was not given a toothbrush. When Pam arrived home that day she found that Mandi, the hygienist during that visit, had given her two toothbrushes, apparently to make up for the one she had been shorted years earlier. Pam freely admits that she was somewhat paranoid about her weight at the time.

On a more serious but happy note, our daughters Sarah and Hillary are both doing well at the time of writing. Sarah's arthritis is currently in remission. She is no longer taking any medication. Although she occasionally tires easily, she plays soccer and loves to ride her bike up the canyon. Sarah is becoming a tall, beautiful, healthy young woman. To look at her you wouldn't suspect the physical struggle she has endured.

Hillary's tumors continue to grow at the same pace her bones are growing. Fortunately the tumors are still benign. They are not very painful, and they have not grotesquely deformed her hand as we had feared they might. She will require surgery some day to remove the largest, most intrusive tumors. Her doctor tells us that she is past the growth stage where the tumors were most likely to rapidly grow. We hope and pray that Hillary will continue to be spared from the more negative potential of her disease.

We are profoundly grateful for the current good health of our children. We are thankful for the good medical care that Sarah and Hillary have received. They continue to have regular visits with their doctors. Whenever we visit Primary Children's Hospital in Salt Lake City we are reminded that many children suffer much more. Our hearts go out to those parents who face the tremendous challenge of watching and helping their children suffer through such terrible physical trials.

As Pam was writing the book she would often tell me how she was struggling to say something in just the right way. I resisted the urge to step in and try to write for her. I recognized that this was her story and she alone needed to tell it. However, I often told her that people would be looking for some grand key to successfully facing life's challenges, particularly weight loss. I asked her over and over, "What is the key?" "What was it that finally enabled you to lose the weight?"

Now that the book is done I can see how wrong I was to try to push Pam toward offering some grand key to weight loss. I find her story incredibly motivating. It makes me want to change some things in my life. It gives me confidence that I can change those things. In the end, I think Pam has done exactly what she set out to do—she has given people hope and faith in themselves. And she has done it by simply telling her story.

The motivating message of Pam's story is that ordinary people can accomplish extraordinary things in life by maintaining a consistent focus on the small root causes of success. Pam went from not being able to run more than a few steps to being able to complete a marathon because she did the little things. She learned to have faith that achieving little successes would lead to the accomplishment of her major goals. She also learned to take great satisfaction in those little successes. I think that's a big part of what kept her going. She was able to savor the satisfaction of success along the journey, not just at the finish line.

In a very real sense, her accomplishment was not losing over one hundred pounds, rather it was stringing together literally thousands of good decisions about what to eat and how much to exercise. For me, the powerfully motivating element of Pam's story is that *anyone* can do those small things that need to be done in order to achieve any significant goal, even a seemingly impossible goal like losing over one hundred pounds and running a marathon.

About the Author

Pamela H. Hansen grew up in Salt Lake City, Utah. She attended the University of Utah and graduated from Brigham Young University with a degree in Elementary Education. Although she has taught first and second grades, as well as adult ESL classes, the majority of her life as a mother has been spent at home. She and her husband, Mark, live in Orem, Utah, where they are raising five children.